Asylum Seekers and Refugees in the Contemporary World

The issue of asylum seekers and refugees is one of the most talked about subjects in contemporary politics, fuelled by extensive coverage in the media. David J. Whittaker's book provides a balanced introduction to this very controversial subject.

Asylum Seekers and Refugees in the Contemporary World discusses the international as well as national implications of the issue, looking at the way different governments have dealt with it. Taking a number of case studies, for example Palestinian, Afghan and Iraqi refugees, Whittaker cuts through the emotive language to give an objective introduction to the subject. The book looks in detail at the issue as it has affected Britain and Europe in particular, as well as including material on the UN and its response to the refugee 'problem'.

Including a final statement on the British government's 2005 proposals for dealing with refugees, *Asylum Seekers and Refugees in the Contemporary World* is essential reading for all students of the history of the modern world and is ideal for newcomers to the subject.

David J. Whittaker is recently retired and was formerly Lecturer in International Relations at the University of Teesside. His many books include *United Nations in Action, Conflict and Reconciliation in the Contemporary World, Terrorists and Terrorism in the Contemporary World*, and *The Terrorism Reader*.

The Making of the Contemporary World
Edited by Eric J. Evans and Ruth Henig

The Making of the Contemporary World series provides challenging interpretations of contemporary issues and debates within strongly defined historical frameworks. The range of the series is global, with each volume drawing together material from a range of disciplines – including economics, politics and sociology. The books in this series present compact, indispensable introductions for students studying the modern world.

Asylum Seekers and Refugees in the Contemporary World
David J. Whittaker

China under Communism
Alan Lawrence

The Cold War
David Painter

Communism and Its Collapse
Stephen White

Conflict and Reconciliation in the Contemporary World
David J. Whittaker

Conflicts in the Middle East since 1945 – 2nd Edition
Beverley Milton-Edwards and Peter Hinchcliffe

Decolonization – Second Edition
Raymond Betts

Dividing and Uniting Germany
J. K. A. Thomaneck and Bill Niven

Globalization
Peter Wardley

The International Economy since 1945
Sidney Pollard

Islamic Fundamentalism since 1945
Beverley Milton-Edwards

Latin America – Second Edition
John Ward

Pacific Asia
Yumei Zhang

The Soviet Union in World Politics
Geoffrey Roberts

States and Nationalism in Europe Since 1945
Malcolm Anderson

Terrorists and Terrorism in the Contemporary World
David J. Whittaker

Thatcher and Thatcherism – 2nd Edition
Eric J. Evans

United Nations in the Contemporary World
David J. Whittaker

The Uniting of Europe – 2nd Edition
Stanley Henig

US Foreign Policy since 1945
Alan Dobson and Steve Marsh

Women and Political Power in Europe since 1945
Ruth Henig and Simon Henig

Asylum Seekers and Refugees in the Contemporary World

David J. Whittaker

Routledge
Taylor & Francis Group

LONDON AND NEW YORK

First published 2006 by Routledge
2 Park Square, Milton Park, Abingdon, Oxon OX14 4RN

Simultaneously published in the USA and Canada
by Routledge
270 Madison Ave, New York NY 10016

Routledge is an imprint of the Taylor & Francis Group

© 2006 David J. Whittaker

Typeset in Times by Taylor & Francis Books
Printed and bound in Great Britain
by MPG Books Ltd, Bodmin, Cornwall

British Library Cataloguing in Publication Data
A catalogue record for this book is available from the British Library

Library of Congress Cataloging in Publication Data
Whittaker, David J., 1925-
  Asylum seekers and refugees in the contemporary world / David J.
Whittaker.
    p. cm. -- (The making of the contemporary world)
  ISBN 0-415-36090-0 (hardback) -- ISBN 0-415-36091-9 (pbk.) 1.
Refugees. 2. Political refugees. 3. Asylum, Right of. I. Title. II. Series.
  HV640.W45 2005
  325'.21--dc22
                              2005014431

ISBN10: 0-415-36090-0   ISBN13: 978-0-415-36090-6 (hbk)
ISBN10: 0-415-36091-9   ISBN13: 978-0-415-36091-3 (pbk)

T&F informa

Taylor & Francis Group is the Academic Division of T&F Informa plc.

Contents

Tables

Preface

The subject addressed in this book has become one of the most talked-about topics in the contemporary world. Equally prominent is some government irresolution and shift and much public ignorance, misunderstanding and prejudice. Many issues are worth exploring – motivation, migrant flows, the economic, social, cultural and legislative aspects of government policies and the fundamentals of public acceptance, rejection and scapegoat.

The book has been designed as a primer, a set of signposts, to help the reader understand, reflect and join others in enquiry. Twelve chapters describe the main issues and four case studies illustrate the complexity and diversity in situation and response. A final retrospect includes a list of crucial points for readers' further discussion.

I am grateful for the ready assistance of many people. At the Refugee Council, Jean Candler answered a number of my queries. At the Information Centre about Asylum and Refugees in the UK (ICAR), located at Kings College, London, Esme Peach was generous with time and the provision of resources and addresses. Carolyn Baker at the European Council for Refugees and Exiles (ECRE), also in London, was a mine of information. The Medical Foundation for the Care of Victims of Torture let me read refugees' testimonies and then reproduce them in my Chapter 11 and for that I am indebted to Jane Spence and Sheila Hayman. Librarians in the universities of Durham and Teesside gave me unstinting help. Marianne Whittaker has helped shed light on psychological aspects of asylum seeking.

As for the hard work in producing a final manuscript, Eve Setch and Alex Ballantine at Routledge have helped me a tremendous amount, and Jane Thompson, once again, has done an excellent job in typing it. Otherwise, any mistakes or misinterpretations are my own responsibility.

David J. Whittaker
Richmond, North Yorkshire

1   Asylum seekers and refugees
Definition, facts, figures

This chapter attempts to trace pathways through the forest of meanings so evident in press and public debate. A number of questions will be considered. In what ways are bona fide refugees and other asylum seekers distinguishable? Fifty years ago an international convention and, later, broadened definitions, set down lines of definition and outlined means of helping the oppressed. A 'well-found fear of persecution' was stated to be a criterion for recognising the refugee. What significance can be given to this as a determining factor? Are there ways in which these meanings and approaches have shifted over the years? Are they still valid in the contemporary world?

Human floods

'Asylum seeker' is a term heard on all sides today, prominent in newsprint and on television screens, discussed everywhere in parliaments, regional assemblies, women's associations and working men's clubs. The meaning the term is given in common parlance is vague, ambiguous, often censorious, and its implications are hotly debated. Over against this difficulty in careful definition is the fearful scenario of millions on the move, in turmoil and danger, deprived of a normal life because of conflict and persecution and pressing inexorably upon the settled communities of the civilised world.

More and more people move around the world than ever before in recorded history, as the next chapter will record. The movements are difficult to gauge with any accuracy but a common estimate is that since 1945 some 50 to 60 million people have been uprooted and left their homes either voluntarily or involuntarily. The so-called 'zones of anguish', from which 'persons of concern' have flooded, were Europe in the 1950s, Africa in the 1960s, Asia in the 1970s and 1980s and, once more, Europe, particularly since the 1990s. These victims of persecution and conflict seek safety and opportunity elsewhere. Today, there are at least 17 million people in transit seeking some form of asylum – over 6 million in Asia, 4.2 million in Africa, and 4.2 million in Europe. These figures will be examined in detail in the next chapter (Tables 2.1 and 2.2). Probably half of these unfortunates are women and children.

It is difficult to calculate the size of the migrant flood in view of its astonishing diversity and changes in its composition. There will be those desperate to get away from persecution and discrimination whom the world will acknowledge as genuine refugees. Others, the economic migrants, will be searching for a better life and prospects elsewhere. Environmental degradation will force many to leave their homes. Great numbers of people are displaced within their own land, victims of war or political coups or ethnic cleansing. Many will be unable to escape to a friendlier country, remaining holed up in temporary camps or inhospitable regions; others will flee abroad, chancing their fate somewhere as illegal immigrants. Overall, with growing ease of travel, the world is a smaller place, with a chance to get away more easily to knock on other doors. Given this diversity, a search for meanings is vital, though forbidding in its complexity and scale.

The search for meaning

There is, then, every reason to do something about mass migration. All manner of issues are raised – humanitarian, ethical, legal, political. In order to act positively there must be a consensus as to the meaning of the terms used.

In 1945 a Specialised Agency of the recently formed United Nations, the United Nations High Commission for Refugees (UNHCR), was given the task in Geneva of framing a tight definition of the term refugee. This would be a modern, legal enactment of the ancient tradition of furnishing asylum to anyone at risk and danger. The definition devised is the one used today, and given the scale and diversity of human movement it remains more than ever necessary to use it to separate very precisely those who are to be distinguished as victims of persecution. A convention was eventually drawn up after seven arduous months of discussion and published by the UNHCR in July 1951 to give the term refugee a very clear definition, namely:

> A person who is outside his/her country of nationality or habitual residence; has a well-founded fear of persecution because of his/her race, religion, nationality, membership of a particular social group or political opinion; and is unable or unwilling to avail

himself/herself of the protection of that country, or to return there, for fear of persecution.

The Convention was to consolidate previous international instruments relating to refugees and would provide a comprehensive codification of basic rights. It must be applied to all without prejudice to race, religion or country of origin.

It was ordained that no application for refugee status would ever be allowed from any person found guilty of committing what was considered to be a war crime or a crime against humanity or a serious non-political offence, or if (in terms thought innovative in 1951) he had been guilty 'of acts contrary to the purposes and principles of the UN'. Such persons were undeserving of international protection and should face justice. (In later years this ruling was to lead to dilemmas for the UNHCR endeavouring to cope with mass streams of people in the Balkans and Central Africa when all too clearly the agents of assassination and genocide must be among those looking for sanctuary.)

There were several essential requirements for refugee validity in the Convention definition of refugee. First, one had to cross a frontier in seeking sanctuary elsewhere, to be recognised as a bona fide refugee. Rather strangely, it seems, the Convention was not to apply to those refugees who were the concern of UN agencies other than UNHCR, such as Palestinian refugees in the Near East (UNRWA). Further, one must be the victim or target of an individual and specific form of harassment; it was not enough to be one of a crowd endeavouring to escape the threat or heat of battle, nor to be merely a member of a group suffering from some form of active discrimination. The life and liberty of an individual was at stake. Second, and quite crucially, there was the existence of a rational and 'well-founded fear' that any return to the country of origin would be impossible, resulting in individual harm. This must go beyond presumption to some proof, and the burden of proof would be upon the claimant, although UNHCR would do its best to scrutinise evidence of a prospective risk. Third, and most importantly,

> No Contracting State shall expel or return [*refouler*] a refugee against his or her own will in any manner whatsoever to the frontier of territories where life or freedom would be threatened on account of his race, religion, nationality, membership of a particular group or political opinion.

It was understood by Convention signatories that they would not be required to give permanent asylum to all refugees but, of course, must do their best to ensure adequate and effective protection. As the next chapter records, this proviso has led to many states granting only temporary protection and to encouraging voluntary repatriation when a second or third state is judged to be a 'safe' harbour.

The last qualification, known as *refoulement*, has been much debated since 1951. Even so, there is general acceptance of its over-riding desirability. Two points have been emphasised both by UNHCR and commentators. In the first place, this ruling must not allow any exception, provided that a claimant is not regarded by a host state as a danger to a community or to any aspect of security. A host state must accord any refugee the same treatment and rights as its nationals receive in respect of legislation, right to property, education, housing, welfare benefits and entry to the professions. A special travel passport would guarantee freedom of movement. No refugee must regard himself as outside the law in a country of refuge. Any transgression of that law would render them liable to deporta-tion, if possible, though, to a 'safe third country' rather than to a state judged unsafe. Second, and crucially, it was to be a refugee's *actions* that would be regarded as hostile by a receiving state rather than any affiliation. Detention, even expulsion, in that case might be the only consequence, although there was to be a right of appeal. (Again, in later years this ruling was to prove troublesome to many governments unsure how far an applicant for asylum was associated with nefarious ideas or schemes.) The Convention was also mindful of the importance of family to a refugee. Governments should take necessary measures to ensure that unity of a family was maintained whenever possible and should take particular care of unaccompa-nied children. For this and other exigencies, adequate welfare services would be most necessary.

The Convention of 1951 only binds those states (Contracting States) that have signed the documents in Geneva and so are party to it. At present, 140 states out of the 190 United Nations member-ship have signed in accord. Non-contracting states include a number of Caribbean and southwest Asian states, but the inclusion in that number of significant political players such as Malaysia, Myanmar (formerly Burma), Pakistan and the United Arab Emirates is rather disconcerting to upholders of fundamental human rights. After all, it could be argued that these states have a duty to cooperate with UNHCR since they are signatories to the United Nations Charter whereby they are obliged to cooperate with the Specialised Agencies.

Broadening definition

Events in the later 1950s and 1960s, when many countries were rent by East-West tensions, political coups, social and religious volatility and inter-ethnic strife, soon pointed to a need for broader definitions to take account of multiple menaces to human rights. The original and basic definition was taken rather further in 1967 in a Protocol Relating to the Status of Refugees. This was related to the 1951 Convention in spirit and format but was an independent instrument. A statement from UNHCR itself affirmed that the Protocol 'fundamentally transformed the 1951 Convention from a document fixed in a specific moment in history into a human rights instrument which addresses contemporary forms of human rights abuse which are properly called persecution'. Certainly the Protocol stressed that the protective regimes of 1951 and 1967 should not be subject to geographical or territorial restrictions or any time restriction but were, in essence, universal in character and operation. The explanation of this ruling is that the Convention drawn up in the immediate aftermath of the Second World War had limited its protective scope mainly to persons who became refugees before 1 December 1951 and as a result of events that had taken place in Europe. Fifteen years later, there was a need to make Convention provisions applicable to the growing numbers of displaced persons everywhere. In every sense, signatory states (States Parties) must undertake undivided cooperation with UNHCR, given that the enactments of 1951 and 1967 were primarily concerned with protection rather than material assistance. (Once more there is a ruling here which was to be overtaken by the sheer scale of material wants of hordes in flight – UNHCR, in liaison with other United Nations agencies and non-governmental organisations, simply had to ensure that refugees remained alive).

Very likely by the mid-1960s such a Protocol was easier to see accepted than in the confusing aftermath of a recent world war. Most major refugee flows were now in the developing world rather than in a lacerated, post-conflict Europe. Decolonisation had brought new states into being and such communities were anxious to stabilise erosion of population and to bring into being schemes for relief for their displaced and disadvantaged people. The industrial states of the developed world were now envisaging programmes for addressing human rights violations on a larger scale. In respect of their evident 'conscience', it has to be said that within such states there were now active and vocal champions of refugee need. Perhaps influential too in bringing into being a more evident public concern for dislodged people was the growth of a civil rights movement in the United States undermining exclusionary practices and calling for a new deal for the world's uprooted. In due course, and by 2003, 145 nations have acceded to the Protocol and now find themselves pledged to a very firm obligation to cooperate with UNHCR in exercising its function of offering a particular individual refugee guaranteed protection, the safeguarding of human rights, a means of transit, and altogether the assurance of an accessible and safe refuge. Signatory states were now given the task of keeping the UN Secretary-General informed as to the extent they were implementing the Protocol through laws, regulations, decrees and actual fieldwork with refugees. Above all, the term *recognised refugee* (the one to be used) had now been given a widely enhanced significance.

Meanings framed in this manner lay upon signatory states an obligation to offer a particular individual protection, the safeguarding of fundamental human rights, the means of transit and the assurance of an accessible and safe refuge. Most importantly, the recognised refugee will expect and be offered a permanent place of safety. Nevertheless, it has been argued, the refugee claimant becomes subject to decisions by states which may rate their own political agendas higher than humanitarian concerns. There is the point, too, that expanding the definition of 'refugee' to include individuals from other endangered groups brings the risk that governments will shut the door on all groups.

What, though, should be done to identify and protect the increasing numbers rendered vulnerable and hapless when political happenings on a grand scale make normal life impossible for an individual, such as has been the case in regions of Africa, in the Balkans and in much of Central and South America? Members of the Organisation of African Union (OAU) came together in 1969 to extend the 1951 definition of refugee, for they were well aware of the unfortunate consequences of civil instability following decolonisation in their new lands. A legitimate understanding of the term 'refugee' would be any person who 'owing to external aggression, occupation, foreign domination or events seriously disturbing public order . . . is compelled to leave his habitual place of residence'. This broader formulation referring to circumstances threatening 'life, physical integrity or liberty' clearly had in mind express provision for persons forced to flee situations of generalised violence and in many ways constituted a mechanism of dealing with en masse refugee movements without individual screening. In north and east Africa at this time there was something of the order of a million people evicted forcibly from their homes. (Again, in later years such movements were to become increasingly common, raising ethical and logistical dilemmas for UNHCR.) A consequence of the expanded definition was that many developing countries anxious to help the oppressed became saddled with a disproportionate burden coping with numbers, material needs and funding. Particularly in Africa, newly independent nations regarded any individual as living within the context of a family as well as a community. A refugee had a responsibility to discharge kinship duties and to maintain family unity if at all possible. Thus, all family members, whether together or separated, should share in a refugee's valid status on a prima facie basis. This unity was stressed in the Protocol more strongly than in the earlier Convention. If the family were separated, there was to be an expectation that they could be reunited. Refugee definitions on the OAU agenda appear to have had in mind collective concepts more than the rights of a lone individual. In some respects, rights in the developed world appear to be based on the concept of autonomous persons giving priority to individual, political and civic rights, where in non-Western traditions there is more emphasis on economic and social entitlement, family obligations and community duties. In any case, whatever the distinctiveness we may give to rights and duties, it is in poor, illiterate societies, especially, that *force majeure*, in the shape of war, starvation and environmental disaster, precipitates refugees.

Asylum seekers

Apart from the term refugee, a word on all lips is that of asylum seeker. Here, meanings are looser. The ancient right of asylum asserted, for instance, in innumerable documents and expressed most vividly by those who lifted the Sanctuary Knocker on Durham Cathedral's great west door, is now interpreted by the oppressed and by observers as both expectation and claim. Moving from Here to There is to be prudent, justifiable and deserving of ready assistance. Generally, in the eyes of authority, an asylum seeker is a person in transit who is applying for sanctuary in some other place than his native land. He is a migrant in search of something better and in that sense is an intending immigrant. He has moved across frontiers, in common with the recognised refugee, but motives and experiences will have to be rigorously examined to see whether or not they meet the strict definition as enacted in the Convention of 1951 and the Protocol of 1967. The implications of being an asylum seeker will be looked at in detail in the next chapter.

Persecution

To understand fully what it is that drives a refugee to flee and seek asylum, it is useful to examine the implications of the term 'persecution'. In 1996 the Council of the European Union sought to harmonise definition of the term 'refugee' with UNHCR, in order that European states could prepare common guidelines for the recognition and admission of persons claiming refugee status. The 'well-founded fear' of persecution had to be appreciated in the light of the circumstances of each case. It is for the asylum seeker to submit the evidence needed to assess the strength of a case, with the additional safeguard that once the credibility of the case has been established the asylum seeker should be given the benefit of the doubt unless there are good reasons to the contrary. The term 'persecution' is notoriously difficult to pin down in definition. The Convention does not do that, nor does UNHCR at all clearly. Nevertheless, there is broad agreement that persecution relates to actions which deny human dignity in any key way through systemic and sustained denial of basic human rights such as are codified, for example, in the Universal Declaration of Human Rights of 1948. What is important here is the extent to which a person deserves international protection because this is not available in the homeland.

Persecution itself is not legally defined but is generally based on persistent and consistent patterns of abuse, intervention and intolerance. Apart from the Universal Declaration, there have been many attempts to set these rights down as incontrovertible and universal. A moment's reflection, however, presents what are termed fundamental rights as subject to conditions and cultural factors; indeed, to a mass of enabling or prescriptive factors. The conventional nostrum that human rights are universal, indivisible, interdependent and interrelated has never looked entirely credible since 1951 (and many never thought it so even then). After all, as many relief workers in disaster areas used to say, 'human rights begin with the availability of breakfast'. Granted that this may be so, one has to start somewhere and one rather basic tabling of rights might be on these lines:

- Freedom from – arbitrary deprivation of life or liberty or movement, inhumane or degrading treatment.
- Freedom to – express thoughts and attitudes in public, to practise social and religious participation, to enjoy fair and equal protection in law, and benefit from socio-economic rights in relation to shelter, jobs, health, education.

Denial of rights and freedoms such as these, where it is deliberate and ongoing, is surely persecution but the term is double-edged. The state has failed to ensure and guarantee protection. Recently, UNHCR even encapsulated this twin relationship in a formula where:

Persecution = the risk of individual serious harm + failure of state protection.

As for state failure to protect, this may be because the state responsible for what is held to be harmful action condones it, tolerates it, or generally either refuses adequate protection or is for some reason unable to offer it. No breach of human rights can be ignored, discounted, or explained away on the basis of culture, tradition or religion. (Frequent violations of basic rights occur in Afghanistan, Myanmar, Saudi Arabia and among Palestinian refugees in Israel.)

For many years, Amnesty International has chronicled spiralling political violence in very many countries which, when it bears down upon certain groups and particularly upon individuals, constitutes persecution. Colombia, Chechnya, Pakistan, Sudan, Congo, Israel, China, North Korea, Uzbekistan, Georgia and Indonesia are countries where arbitrary detention has furnished a host of 'prisoners of conscience' and, for those who escape, a revelation that physical abuse including torture is either a sustained means of dealing with those who dissent on moral grounds, or episodic, so leading to mental breakdown, attempted escape, even suicide. A particular difficulty for a claimant and often for UNHCR investigators is that persecution may well be a form of behaviour whose exact instigators are difficult to trace. Is a government to be held responsible for violations and abuses committed constantly or from time to time by its security forces or by independent agents? Governments, and, indeed, their agents are unlikely to admit guilt and may even act claiming some degree of impunity. How far is it possible to shame, as it were, a government into redressing human rights violations when an escaped refugee provides full and impartial evidence of ill treatment, 'disappearances', arrest and detention? Another complex point for a refugee claimant to assert is that 'well-founded fear' is in one sense hypothetical. It is quite possible that a fear of persecution need not necessarily exist at the time of an asylum seeker's leaving his country of origin (Amnesty International's reports give plenty of substance to this). A well-founded fear, as the term suggests, may be based on the fact that circumstances in country of origin have deteriorated so much since he left that a return would have the gravest of consequences.

Discrimination on its own is not an established case for refugee status, although it is often cited as an instance of deliberate persecution. Where it leads to genocide, as it did in Central Africa and the Balkans, there is an unanswerable case for swift and decisive refugee protection. Persons considering themselves as being treated less fairly than others may have an understandable grievance but they are not necessarily victims of persecution, unless it can be proven that their ethnic or religious or political characteristics are used to set them apart at a disadvantage. A measure of a selective approach to a community for whom a state is responsible will exist in many societies to a greater or lesser degree. It was never easy for UNHCR to mediate at the time of political persecution in the Soviet Union when a 'dissenter' might be arrested and charged for waywardness and refused permission to emigrate. Nor could a supposedly neutral United Nations effectively intervene when from other Eastern Bloc states, countries in Central and South America and in Africa there was a steady exit of dissatisfied 'deviationists'. Their case brought liberal support in most Western countries, which then could support the freedom journey of someone such as Solzhenitsyn, Nureyev or Rostropovitch, but they were never refugees in the care of UNHCR.

Definition and definers

A well known aphorism tells us that the validity of a definition depends to a great extent on the perspectives employed by those who use the definition. This has given the objective decision-making of the UNHCR a great deal of trouble, above all during the Cold War era between 1945 and 1989. A bipolar world generally saw the political and defensive confrontation of the Soviet Bloc and the capitalist West as a meeting of good and evil. There was a political imperative serving the geopolitical interests of the United States and its allies to 'save' as many as possible from perdition. There was a moral duty on the part of a Free World to salvage refugees. Dollars flowed to subsidise the practical provision of liberating channels and contacts. Funds and oratorical campaigning supported liberating agencies such as the US Escapee Program: they did not underwrite the work of UNHCR but sidelined what was taken to be too neutral an institution. It was the Hungarian Uprising of 1956 that saw on the part of the major powers the beginnings of a shift from overt strategic designs countering threat to more concern for the hapless and the oppressed. Both UNHCR and the West could resort to large-scale relief programmes, stepping aside from narrower political criteria. There was, naturally, a political, ideological component in the saving of Hungarians, but more importantly a consensus to launch a major humanitarian undertaking to protect refugees whose validity was incontestable. Henceforth, UNHCR felt able to assume a more vigorous profile and move out of suspicion and near-penury into 'good offices' initiatives that brought it commendation and material support.

Wherever possible, repatriation of refugees was resorted to, depending upon an assessment of whether circumstances in a particular country had improved sufficiently to guarantee 'safe return'.

It is not likely that any United Nations agency can totally avoid engagements in the political sphere. The mere existence of refugees is the result of political upheaval somewhere and, following recognition of relief need (which may be disputed by an unstable country), there will be moves to rescue those in danger. It has become all too clear that humanitarian work cannot act as substitute for political action. Often this leads to Geneva directly standing up to states which will not risk their general interests being impugned. Hallmarks of so much UNHCR work over the years are fine-tuned political sensitivity, ready mediation in difficult circumstances, and a readiness to convince governments that certain solutions are fair and practicable. Where the Cold War years bisected political allegiances fundamentally into East and West, more recent multipolar decades have presented those who would legitimate their efforts for refugees with a host of questions. How far is it possible for external pressures to reduce persecution within a sovereign state? This helped to bring about the crumbling of apartheid, but Amnesty International has for many years been wrestling with the possibilities and limitations of helping an individual-in-need from the outside. The field staff of UNHCR would not want the world to regard them as workers in a soup kitchen. Inevitably, even with the original 1951 definition, now somewhat refined, there are judgements to be made and held in context.

Fifty years on

A British former Home Secretary, Jack Straw, commented in 1999 that the 1951 Covenant 'is no longer working as its framers intended'. He had in mind, so he said, the mass flows in the contemporary world from almost every continent and the sheer impossibility of dealing adequately with those internally displaced, with those traumatised in transit, and with illegal immigrants crossing the English Channel. A worrying concern to governments such as his own is the circumstance where intending asylum seekers construct a plea for protection and cast around to see which state is likely to consider their claim for refugee status. Inevitably, the business of processing claims, by any government, becomes complex, costly and subject to much delay and uncertainty. Unfortunately, in the flood of immigration and the inevitable processing queues, there may be scant agreement as to designation, appropriate treatment and destination of applicants. Refugees may spend some time, as it were, 'in orbit', knocking on closing doors.

Another recent view of the 1951 Convention is that of Britain's Prime Minister, Tony Blair, speaking in 2002 to the House of Commons in response to questions about his country's legislation apropos asylum seekers. 'The values of the Convention are timeless', he declared, yet it was now time, 'to stand back and consider its application in today's world'. He must have had in mind the controversy over what has been called in some liberal quarters, 'an eclectic mix of cultures'. His questioners in the Commons, according to Parliamentary reports, were clearly probing the problems of asylum seeker admittance and reception in a world where borders were closing, legal barriers erected, quotas imposed. A refugee today may be asking for legitimate sanctuary elsewhere than in a country torn apart by militias, separatist rebels, paramilitary bands, bandits, mafia, and irresolute governments. Who is to say what persecution means in such places and whether or not it is 'well-founded'?

The following chapter will move from definition and theoretical positions to the field of active, progressive dealing with problem people. Fifty-three years after the Convention was written, the contemporary world is full of enormous challenges, hopes and fears. Constructive action for fairness and victim relief is happening all the time and we would do well to keep in mind the basic vulnerability of both the refugee and the would-be protector. The point was nicely made in December 2001 in Geneva by Vaira Vike-Freiberga, President of Latvia, herself a refugee in the immediate post-war years: she was speaking at a ministerial meeting to consider the 1951 Convention and its Protocol:

No one leaves their home willingly or gladly . . . it means that there is something deeply wrong with the circumstances in their country. And we should never take lightly this plight of refugees fleeing across borders. They are signs, they are symptoms, they are proof that something is very wrong somewhere on the international scene . . . And I like to think that I stand here today as a survivor who speaks for all those who died by the roadside . . . And for all those millions across the world today who do not have a voice, who cannot be heard. They are also human beings, they also suffer, they also have their hopes, their dreams and their aspirations. Most of all they dream of a normal life.

I entreat you . . . when you think about the problem of refugees to think of them not in the abstract. Do not think of them in the bureaucratic language of 'decisions' and 'declarations' and 'priorities' . . . I entreat you, think of the human beings who are touched by your decisions. Think of the lives who wait on your help.

(Feller *et al.* 2003: pp. 44–5)

2 Searchers after asylum

An international problem

Protection of asylum seekers is the concern of this chapter. An outline of the scale of a global problem is followed by a brief glance at asylum seeking through the centuries. Basic principles of individual and group protection will be discussed as a forerunner to considering means of problem resolution current today. When, though, is a refugee no longer a refugee? What is involved in the approach of 'managed migration' as the most effective way of coping with human displacement?

The march of millions

Accurate statistics are difficult to calculate given the size and disparity and changing nature of asylum seeking. The hapless people themselves are wrestling with problems of identity, security and sheer day-to-day existence: the task of enumeration and distinction is certainly problematic for anyone attempting to gauge its extent. Nevertheless, UNHCR and the Refugee Council in London are able to publish what amounts to a generalised survey of a globalised situation, and it is these rounded-off and provisional figures which will be quoted in this and other chapters.

At the start of the year 2004, the number of 'people of concern' to UNHCR was 17.1 million. This is actually down from 21.8 million in 2000 and 20.6 million in 2003. This total is estimated to include 9.7 million refugees (57 per cent), 985,500 asylum seekers (6 per cent), 1.1 million returned refugees (6 per cent), 4.4 million internally displaced persons (26 per cent) and 912,000 others of concern (5 per cent). (The meaning of some of these terms will be explained later in this chapter.)

The number of uprooted persons fell by 17 per cent to 17.1 million in 2003, the lowest total in at least a decade. It reflected both increased international efforts to find solutions for uprooted people and positive developments in some parts of the world where there was an end to long-sustained conflicts.

The global refugee total decreased from 10.6 million to 9.7 million, largely on account of the return of almost 650,000 Afghans from Pakistan and Iran (another 2 million of them, however, are still in exile). Asian numbers were down by 30 per cent. Latin America and the Caribbean increased their numbers chiefly because of 1.2 million displaced by civil war in Colombia.

Although overall refugee numbers are now less, there were almost 290,000 new refugees registered in 2003. Large mass exits occurred from Sudan (112,000), Liberia (86,600), the Democratic Republic of the Congo (30,000), Côte d'Ivoire (22,200), Somalia (14,800) and the Central African Republic (13,000).

The chief hosting countries giving shelter to refugees are Pakistan (1.1 million), Iran (985,000), Germany (960,000), Tanzania (650,000) and the United States (452,500). All five of these saw declines in refugee numbers of between 2 and 25 per cent. Asia became a host to more than a third of all the people of concern to UNHCR, giving sanctuary to 6.2 million people or 36 per cent, followed by Africa, 4.3 million (25 per cent), Europe, 4.2 million (25 per cent), Latin America, 1.3 million (8 per cent), North America, 978,100 (5 per cent) and Oceania, 74,400 (0.4 per cent).

During 2003, 809,000 people all over the world applied for asylum. Combined with applications still unprocessed from earlier years, the grand total awaiting decision was 985,000 at the end of 2003. Iraqi nationals had been the largest single group of claimants in 2002.

Table 2.1 Persons of concern to UNHCR – by region

Region	1 Jan. 2003	1 Jan. 2004
Asia	9,378,900	6,187,800
Africa	4,593,200	4,285,100
Europe	4,403,900	4,242,300
North America	1,061,000	978,100
Latin America and Caribbean	1,050,300	1,316,400
Oceania	69,200	74,400
Total	20,556,700	17,084,100

Source: UNHCR, *Refugees by Numbers*, 2003 edition

The number of people receiving assistance once they had gone back home – 'returnees' – stood at 1.1 million in 2003, down from 2.4 million in 2002.

The magnitude of the task facing the world in respect of protecting asylum seekers is demonstrated in Tables 2.1 and 2.2.

Something else constituting 'persons of concern' is a gender factor, the proportion of male to female in all these sad figures. It is generally estimated that between 75 and 80 per cent of refugees are women and children. They are not only the dependent ones in families but they are clearly the most vulnerable. Eight out of ten casualties from small weaponry are women and children. Many of the women suffer abuse at the hands of invaders. Females and adolescents easily fall into the hands of traffickers who prey upon those with little security, and they may be coerced into sexual slavery. The Convention of 1951 did not even consider the issue of gender protection. Female persecution for the first time reached the statute books in 1984 when the European Parliament took a revolutionary step towards codifying equal rights. Member states were asked to consider women as a distinctive social group who would often have an urgent case for claiming refugee status.

Asylum seeking through the ages

There is nothing new in the situation of an individual or of a crowd seeking safety, comfort and reassurance. For thousands of years, exiles have attempted to exchange persecution for freedom. What is relatively new is that their troubled conscience and desperation have engendered an international and compassionate move to do something for them systematically. Most of us are well aware of the press of people

Table 2.2 Estimated number of refugees and persons of concern to UNHCR worldwide

Year	Refugees	Total population of concern
1999	11,687,000	20,624,000
2000	12,130,000	21,871,000
2001	12,117,000	19,871,000
2002	10,594,000	20,691,000
2003	9,672,000	17,084,100

looking for something better or even for a guarantee of life. Some of the more dramatic asylum searches are these:

- Fifteenth century   Moors, Jews, expelled from Spain by the Inquisition.
- Seventeenth century Puritans cross the Atlantic seeking religious freedom.
- Eighteenth century   French aristocrats flee the French Revolution.
- Nineteenth century   Russians, Poles, Germans flee autocracies.
- 1918   Pogroms, revolution, ethnic strife in Russia, Balkans, Asia Minor, lead to individual émigrés and large-scale movements as revolutions topple dynasties.
- 1930s   Fascist repression and aggression evict many from Germany, Italy, Spain, China.
- Second World War   Estimated 7 million Jews, Gypsies, political dissidents ill treated, even liquidated, by Nazis.
- 1945–56   Over 200,000 Poles, Czechs, Latvians, Lithuanians, Hungarians, welcomed to Britain as 'volunteer workers' fleeing Soviet oppression.
- 1950s   Communist takeover of Tibet, China, Indonesia, Castro in Cuba, and Israeli-Arab wars, lead to wholesale evictions and flight.
- 1960s, 1970s   Vietnam War displaces many thousands.
- 1974   Cyprus is divided, with 200,000 Greek Cypriots moving south, 40,000 Turkish Cypriots going north. Division seems set in stone.
- 1980s–2000   Liberation struggles, wars, coups, ethnic contests, environmental disasters, poverty, famines, all generate mass movements, e.g. Ugandan Asians, Chileans, Kurds, Zaireans, former Yugoslavs.

Jews, particularly, have long been exiles, victimised and ousted. Their dispersion, the diaspora, has been a feature of history since Roman persecution in first-century Palestine. For centuries, those who did not flee were confined to ghettoes, exposed to anti-Semitism and atrocity. After 1945 many thousands of Jews were able to settle in Israel, their Promised Land. Jewish refugees everywhere have made an incomparable contribution to the arts, to literature, to music and to science.

Thus we have a history of individual and group retreat from persecution and hardship meeting a counter-response whether of acknowledgement, reception, welcome, assimilation and integration or of bureaucratic obstruction and popular prejudice. In general terms, as we have already noted, there appears to have been a move to coordinate a humanitarian and helpful response to asylum seeking. It could be said that even the most unhelpful and least compassionate of observers increasingly admit that the scale and diversity of mass emigration now calls for planned and consistent handling if the settled world is not to become ever more chaotic. Even so, many informed critics of this 'handling' by European governments see states' policies as ever more restrictive, coloured by short-sightedness, sectional interests and hypocrisy. The rest of this chapter will take a close look at the matter of protection for asylum seekers – the principles underlying international approach, some of the means commonly employed to manage migration, and, finally, the prospects of preventive action. Throughout the discussion there will be references to controversy and to issues calling for attention and solution.

Protection principles

A number of critical principles are basic and are generally observed, namely:

- Sovereign states together with international institutions have responsibility for helping and protecting asylum seekers in what should be a planned and coordinated fashion. Generally, this replaces the earlier diplomatic and consular system which may be unable or unwilling to assist.
- A protection system must take account of claimants' present, past and likely future experiences.
- Claimants cannot always expect indefinite leave to remain in asylum until their identity is fully established.
- Claimants are to be guaranteed treatment without any discrimination and with the absolute right of non-refoulement.

Principles such as these underscore the common practices in dealing with asylum claims that are adopted by most states today. There will be a description and discussion of this in the shape of a number of case studies in following chapters.

The contemporary world is volatile, unpredictable and challenging. How far, then, can field workers with asylum seekers keep fundamental principles always firmly in focus? The evidence shows this to be taxing, given that principles such as those above are to govern the first essential stage in processing, and that is to grant an applicant discretionary leave to remain.

Erika Feller, UNHCR's Director of the Department of International Protection, outlined a number of burning problems in an address to the 51st Session, UNHCR's Executive Committee in Geneva, in 2001 (UNHCR website, Protecting Refugees). In the first place, every continent now has to cope with some mass exodus. Here and there, a warring conflict is unresolved, contending parties bitterly wrestle for supremacy, there is no real legitimate authority and scant observance of humanitarian norms. Conflicts overlap frontiers and neighbouring states are understandably anxious about their own security as well as any possibility of meeting the material needs of large numbers of dependent incomers. For these states to steer close to principles constitutes a challenge which can lead to 'asylum seeker fatigue' and a defensive aborting of provision. Consultation and encouragement will have to come from the outside, provided that no state feels it is ordered what to do. Second, there is the growing difficulty of distinguishing, in the hordes, who is legitimate refugee and who may be opportunistic migrant. Working out these distinctions amid dust and debacle results often in frustration, restricted access, limitation of benefits and curtailment of rights. Third, and a consequence of the foregoing lack of clarity, how do we deal with migrants who deliberately misuse asylum seeker processes? Too sternly impeding their access may adversely affect chances of acceptance by legitimate refugees. Last, for Feller, no time is to be lost in establishing an inter-states framework to push forward half-realised objectives, to sort out claimants, to process their applications as quickly as possible, to deal with errant claimants, and to speed on to safety those who are judged as needing it. In the course of this standardisation it will be supervisory teams that are counselled, trained and their work monitored with as little as possible left to chance. Partnership between states and non-governmental organisations (NGOs) is a crucial step towards a straightening out and thorough improvement of procedures.

For Erika Feller a reform process leads to an inescapable conclusion:

> An agenda for protection, therefore, must be firmly grounded in a principled approach that refugee protection is first and foremost about meeting the needs of vulnerable and threatened individuals, but to be effective, it must take into account the exigencies of the environment in which protection must be delivered, including the rights and interests of states and host communities.

Another problem, not mentioned by Feller but frequently voiced at UNHCR sessions in Geneva, is the life-threatening challenge of much work in conflict situations. Principles and programmes are fine if humanitarian workers are themselves protected from the bullet and the bomb. In West Timor, Guinea and Iraq, would-be rescuers have paid with their lives in getting access to those they were mandated to protect.

People of 'major concern'

Unquestionably, it is the uprooted mass of émigrés that has put principles and practice into question at times. The people of 'major concern' over several decades now are the Internally Displaced Persons, the 'IDPs'. They are those who stayed in their homeland, besieged and bereft, urgently needing help and some form of extrication for sanctuary. There are 4.4 million of them spread over several continents. In some ways their plight exceeds that within the remit of the 1951 Covenant and the later 1967 Protocol where it is necessary to distinguish valid refugees from others on the move. How can these people best be rescued?

Originally, the term 'Displaced Persons' was coined towards the end of the Second World War to denote those anguished survivors from Nazi forced labour camps or the dazed exiles from Soviet-occupied territories. A huge relief operation by Allied armies and the new United Nations revitalised almost 5 million people and returned them to their homes. Another million were unwilling to reside under communist control, many of the 'unfree' (and 'useful allies') finding their way to Britain or to the United States, usefully importing brain- and manpower into the booming West. Seventy-two other countries opened their doors to 200,000 'DPs'.

In today's world there are an estimated 4.4 million people who have been uprooted and dispossessed within their own country. Three out of four Palestinian Arabs have been uprooted in Israel over fifty years. There are others in Indochina. Nepal, Bangladesh, or Sri Lanka, who tend to be forgotten as the media highlights yet another crisis elsewhere. They stay, perhaps ignored, in the land they know rather than cross a frontier. Sadly, their status is not covered within the confines of international law: they owe what recovery comes along to the 'good offices' of UNHCR or that of some state or NGO sympathetic to their misery. Even worse is the reality, ever more obvious today, that they are not always welcome as immigrants in settled lands. How will they cope with a search for housing and jobs? Can they bring themselves to understand the niceties of customs and the law?

A way out for the displaced in limbo is to opt for voluntary repatriation, as we shall see shortly. Voluntary return to the place they know best is a risky prospect but it may be the most practicable solution for both victim and aid agency. During 2003 and into 2004, well over a million 'returnees' have decided to chance things and go back to Afghanistan, Angola, Iraq, Sri Lanka, Eritrea, Congo, Namibia, Colombia and the Balkans, thus markedly reducing numbers of asylum seekers. The United Nations has devised a number of so-called Quick Action Projects (QAPs) to assist those going back into local communities, either as familiar figures or as strangers. Practical help with money grants, skills teaching, and rebuilding of homes, schools and infrastructure will help incomers find their feet and lead perhaps to quicker and more welcome reception by those who stayed behind. Counselled by team workers from the UN's specialised agencies, returnees choose their own priorities, elect leaders, and manage their own way of working.

Unhelpfully, a number of these returner schemes for bringing the displaced back to their original homes are bedevilled by the fact that conflict resolution is often hard to achieve and reconciliation, that extra mile, even more difficult to see established.

Voluntary repatriation

Undoubtedly, most refugees prefer a return home, as soon as circumstances allow this, when a conflict is at an end and some semblance of normal life is a prospect. Governments with a mass influx heading in their direction are easily persuaded that an assisted passage home is better than a half-life endured in an overcrowded camp. Observers of the trauma felt by those who come back to desolation are not so sure that these people can cope without the safety net of carefully planned rehabilitation programmes. Safety, in itself, is a vague term. In a war-to-peace transition, such as took many months to develop in Cambodia, Mozambique and Bosnia, governance and the social fabric are in tatters. Destruction and disillusion abound and there can be nobody much who is able to offer any guarantees of progress and security. After all, in Kosovo, Rwanda, Eritrea, who is my neighbour? Is he a fellow victim or a participant, a 'freedom fighter' armed to the teeth? Did he have any part in violation of human rights such as 'ethnic cleansing'? Might he even have designs on my property or my land? Who is to protect me once the institutional protection framework has left me behind? Which is the safer place to return to – the big city (with or without a ghetto for a minority people) or thinly settled countryside?

Critics cite two examples of what they regard as premature repatriation. In the early 1990s, as the first Gulf War ended, half a million Kurds from Northern Iraq attempted to enter Turkey to get away from the atrocities that the dictator Saddam Hussein had been responsible for. Turkish border guards refused these exiles entry. A hasty redeployment scheme, 'Operation Provide Comfort', penned the Kurds in an inhospitable enclave inside Iraq's far north under the eyes of the US Army, safe, indeed, but almost entirely destitute with no cultivable land and no skills to find an alternative to near-starvation. Comfort was no real solution to anything. Another instance of over-hasty population shifting was the despatch of 100,000 who were evicted from Sierra Leone's fratricide in the year 2000 and taken in convoy to a desolate part of Guinea. Of course, voluntary repatriation has diminished the numbers of uprooted people, despite conjecture as to their settled welfare. Prospects of a brighter life for voluntary repatriates are never going to be sure, and this is more so where volunteers have been, as it were, forced into making a choice. Things can go badly wrong, then, as happened when Tanzania forced Rwandans home in 1996. This sorry story will be told below in Chapter 8.

Temporary protection

Repatriation for some years has been seen as a hit-and-miss operation where there has been too little success to make it a dependable solution to dealing with large numbers. It was in 1992, when the Balkans were in flames and thousands of people were forced out of their homes, that the alternative of 'temporary protection' headed the protection agenda. There seemed every chance that governments might be persuaded to be more generous in their response to large-scale emigration, if they were assured that the tentative protection they were able to offer was compatible with humane principles, but also that it would be short term without the ensuing problems of complex screening and settlement. More obviously, even a drip-feed of short-term relief would save reception from being overloaded and also save on the expenses of elaborate provision, and it could be seen by the public and by the media as a ready response and a practicable one to human catastrophe.

If there was agreement among states to take this solution on board, there was much less consensus about how to rescue the internally displaced from persecution within a sovereign state. How far would it be possible to prevent wholesale violation of human rights in the warring regions of former Yugoslavia? Would extracting some of the victims of 'ethnic cleansing' act as a provocation to the cleansers and prolong conflict? In the wake of such an interventionist action, how could peace and some form of reconciliation ever be restored? Questions such as these were aired widely, and strong opinions abounded that UNHCR had 'sold out' to nations' self-interest and had trimmed policies to a frosty wind in Europe's capitals. There had been a trade-off between UNHCR doing its best by way of Convention principles and states' agreement to carry through a rough and ready, minimalist operation. How 'temporary' could 'temporary' ever be, given the scale and nature of the disruption in Balkan or African areas and the all too obvious impossibility of any prompt and safe return for those evicted?

Criticism was met by UNHCR in Geneva with ready assurances on the lines of 'temporary protection shall not prejudge recognition of refugee status under the Convention' and 'a person enjoying temporary protection must be able to lodge an application for asylum status at any time'. However, it would never be possible for UNHCR to interfere in the hastily streamlined procedures and rather primitive casework that mass reception made inevitable. Some developments appeared disturbing, particularly when, to ease admission procedures, an asylum application was suspended with the likely consequence of lowered entitlement to social and civic rights. Many Bosnian asylum seekers found that even the grant of elemental provision for housing and social welfare was tied to being accommodated in crowded reception centres. Their travel was often restricted.

From time to time, states have agreed a quota programme, where large numbers of the oppressed in a particular region may be admitted to safety. In 1979, sixty-five nations offered sanctuary to hundreds of thousands of Vietnamese seeking to leave the horrors of war in leaky boats. One million of these 'boat people' were taken into hasty sanctuary and eventually resettled globally. A rather tentative British response took only about 20,000, relying heavily on the voluntary sectors. Others were less fortunate, together with many Cambodians, and were condemned to languish under Red Cross emergency care in ghettos in Thailand or Hong Kong. Many of these unfortunates are still there.

Cessation of refugee status

There is much discussion about repatriation and a certain amount of dissatisfaction with the ways in which displaced persons are treated. Inevitably, it is the final resolution of an asylum seeker's status that leads to conjecture, even controversy. When is a refugee no longer a refugee? The terminology of the 1951 Convention is rather guarded and abstract, and a clearer definition of the process known as *cessation* is to be found in a statement from UNHCR's Executive Committee Conclusion No. 69 (XLIII):

> States must carefully assess the fundamental character of the changes in the country of nationality or origin, including the general human rights situation, as well as the particular cause of fear of persecution, in order to make sure in an objective and verifiable way that the situation which has justified the granting of refugee status has ceased to exist.

In compliance with the spirit of this statement it may be thought that a complete political transformation of a country of origin is too much to be hoped for, certainly in the short term. The UNHCR statement further emphasises that the resumption of such factors as an independent judiciary and the upholding of an individual's rights to freedom of liberty, association, movement, expression, peaceful assembly and of access to the rule of law may be a lengthy and uneven business. What are termed 'ceased circumstances' must depend upon developments in a country which are substantial in character, effective in being much more than a promise of improvement and, above all, durable. Such are the circumstances which a careful opinion will rate as terminating a refugee's dependency status. All too clearly, there are risks and assumptions here, however objective the process of considering them is held to be. Will a state receiving repatriates, for instance, be willing to reabsorb those who need housing, transport and jobs, when such things are in short supply for those who stayed (perhaps without protest)? In a sense, clearing the way for cessation of an individual's need of asylum is a search by everybody for guarantees.

Another approach to cessation, often in association with the factors outlined above, is to take into account significant developments in the refugee's own circumstances which point to status and care as no longer appropriate. Factors such as these would have an important bearing on the case:

* Acquisition of a new nationality.
* Reacquisition of a former nationality.
* Voluntary repatriation (whether or not premature).
* Being specifically accepted and put on a democratic electoral roll in their native state.

Cessation of refugee status not only clears an individual of dependency need, it clears whole groups as well, where their original country can now be considered entirely liberated from oppression and persecution. Accordingly, refugees are not expected to come from South Africa, Slovakia, Albania, Namibia, Bulgaria, Romania, Bolivia, Nigeria, Argentina, Uruguay, Czechoslovakia, Hungary or Chile. This is a long list. Many will regard it as attestation of an ever-more tolerant world. No subscriber to Amnesty or to human rights campaigns is likely to be quite that optimistic. *Plus ça change.*

Managed migration

Amid the controversies, claims and counter-claims surrounding the issue of how best to cope with asylum seeker floods, there is from time to time a period of thoughtful reflection and the implementation of consensual policies which are considered fair, constructive and unhurried. A term such as 'managed migration' describes a rational and positive way of dealing with a phenomenal doubling of migration in the last twenty years. Sixty per cent of the movement is in the world's developed lands; 40 per cent in the less developed world. Migration should no longer be seen as merely egress from one place, via transit across another, to arrival elsewhere, resulting in variable and disputed reception practices. Migration, growing astronomically, is increasingly becoming an international problem demanding international management. There is doubt as to whether contemporary policies and practices really address the root causes of migration or provide real security to those who need it. At the heart of the migration phenomenon is the core difficulty of sorting the legitimate refugee from the others but, that apart, now is the time to stop seeing the migrant as an interloper or scapegoat, the Great Unwashed, and to begin looking at the benefits that better management could bring. What is needed is a more holistic view of what migrants need, deserve, and, as the UN Charter affirms, have a right to.

Kofi Annan, the United Nations Secretary-General, in a November 2003 lecture at Columbia University, USA, saw the management challenge as threefold: 'to better protect the human rights of migrants, to fairly share the burdens and responsibilities of providing assistance for refugees, and to fully realize the positive potential of international migration – for migrants and for transit and receiving countries alike'. He conceded that international migration puts into high profile many sensitive issues for governments, to do with economic, political and demographic consequences, social and cultural change, and the allocation of resources. Annan referred to the net benefits that emigration brings. Unemployment and population pressures in the developing world are relieved. Remittances sent home by migrants working in the developed lands total more than the amounts sent as official development aid to their countries of origin. It is reckoned that these funds augment GDP by some 10 per cent in such countries as Jamaica, Jordan and Yemen. Migrants provide a reservoir of cheap labour in the receiving countries, taking up semi-skilled jobs that others avoid. They help to fill the vacuum created in Europe and North America by an ageing population. These all seem rather materialist considerations and they appear to be the ones given most priority in both sender and host countries. Certainly, for the United Nations and liberal thinkers everywhere, there is the ethical point that better management of emigration could do a great deal more to create economic opportunities in poor countries so that people there have an incentive and the wherewithal to stay. A 'well-founded' fear of starvation and destitution must be a powerful motive to escape.

Asylum seekers and security

In the last two decades, the cocktail mix of apprehension, misunderstanding, root prejudice and xenophobia has sharpened attitudes of exclusion among governments and the public at large, and encouraged a closed door response to migration in many quarters, with the rights of migrants and, crucially, of refugees being eroded in the process. In much of contemporary Europe, asylum seekers are regarded as a burden on the state and as a threat to political and economic stability. These are Marginal People, the focus of suspicion and increasing hostility. Their admission and reception need control and direction. Now, during the last three years, and most certainly after 9/11, there is the fear of terrorist admission, a contingency sometimes expressed in apocalyptic terms. Again, there is talk of 'management' with, this time, an incentive for most states to receive, temporarily protect, process and return the immigrant, that is, if tightening security controls can screen out the undesirable. Europe-wide there is increasing anxiety and more rigorous restriction, with immigration procedures limiting access, subsequent movement and even right of appeal. In many respects, as Chapter 4 will describe, it is a fortress posture and set of actions. It is understandable that the United States takes most to heart any prospect of terrorist infiltration and attack. Joanne van Selm, an authority on migration issues, writes recently of an America preoccupied with defending itself against further outrage, passing through Congress in 2001 a raft of stern anti-terrorist measures significantly entitled the USA Patriot Act (Steiner *et al.* 2003: 237ff). A heavy battery of intensive and wide-searching forensic devices was hoisted into place. The questions in the minds of immigration inspectors were very much to the point. 'Who are these people?' 'What do they want?' 'Can we afford to take the risk of letting them in?' Predictably, refugee admission suffered. Yet, as Selm points out, 'Refugees are among the most scrutinised migrants in the world – they are not offering a service for which there is a marked demand, as many economic migrants do, but are arriving, or seeking to flee, because they have nothing'. Stringent checks and procedures will be essential to protect both state and refugee, but for Selm one question must be answered. She asks, 'Do states want to sacrifice the right to seek and enjoy asylum and the principle of non-refoulement on the "combating terrorism pyre"?' This is a sacrifice they must never make.

Protection and prevention

There is common agreement internationally that in order to protect asylum seekers and refugees we must stand by the principles of fifty years ago and fit them into the perspectives of a very different world, the contemporary one. We must look closely into the reasons why people migrate in order to understand, control and, so far as possible, attempt to slacken the flow. Global Consultations, workshops and conferences in Geneva or Lisbon, Cambridge and San Remo are working out schemes for partnerships and networks. In the words of Ruud Lubbers, the Dutch High Commissioner for Refugees (addressing UNHCR Executive Committee in Geneva, 2002), 'pro-active engagement must supersede reactive working'. A Convention Plus will elaborate on the spirit of 1951 and go way beyond it in harnessing a wealth of experience and initiative among states and NGOs. For the asylum seekers en route there will be carefully managed schemes of relief and self-help. Prevention is to have top priority, with projects in such volatile places as Sierra Leone, Sri Lanka and Eritrea seeking to stabilise and reinvigorate communities and so deter those who might leave. A question always tops the agenda: 'do we help them leave or help them stay?' For those lands in trouble, there is to be a bridging of the 'gap' between immediate, emergency aid and long-term, inching-forwards development. As for those who wish to return after emigration (voluntary or forced), there will be a '4R' programme – repatriation, reintegration, rehabilitation, reconstruction. They and their sponsors will be partners in this scheme. Lubbers sees this as 'bringing safety to people rather than people to safety'.

Finally, if we are setting out to protect asylum seekers effectively and to control migration flows, it can only be by means of carefully thought out international management. A recent statement by UNHCR puts this in rounded terms:

> The effectiveness of international refugee protection in years to come hinges on the ability of States and the international community to address [these] challenges whether they involve strategies to separate armed elements in refugee camps, to manage complex migration flows, or to realize durable solutions to the plight of refugees. These initiatives are in turn part of the intricate mosaic of international cooperation which needs to be strengthened if the international community is to address wider economic, social and political problems in refugee-producing countries, global inequities, small arms trade, and so on, which can all lead to the forced displacement of populations within and beyond national borders. To succeed, such international cooperative endeavours require the involvement of all actors, from governments, civil society, international organizations, the legal profession, and NGOs to refugees themselves.
>
> (Feller *et al.* 2003: p. 43)

3 Asylum seekers in Britain
Facts and debate

This chapter, opening with a glance at a number of current media assertions, goes on to present some statistics of immigration into Britain. Reception procedures, underwritten by government policies, are considered, followed by an outline of proposals from non-governmental organisations for improving the ways in which UK asylum seekers have been handled. Legal approaches and measures are discussed in some detail, together with the debatable issues they raise. In conclusion, the problems of resettlement and integration are looked at in general terms, together with an account of one or two provincial programmes and projects taking shape in a world where exploitation abounds. Finally, Britain is seen to face an overriding question in regard to asylum claimants. Is there a system ultimately more responsive to their needs, and one promoting their deserved protection, or is it one that stresses deterrence and control rather than welfare provision and assurance of rights? Have the British succeeded in being appropriately Tender and Tough? (Readers are reminded at this point that systemic circumstances can change dramatically – the scenario described in this chapter is that of autumn 2004. Updating can readily be done through visiting the websites listed at the end of this book.)

A web of fallacies and confusions

Perspectives in today's media are often misinformed, prejudiced and frequently virulent. 'Why do we let in so many spongers?' queried the *Daily Mail* in 1998. The *Sun*, two years later, resented 'the scroungers, beggars and crooks who are prepared to cross every country in Europe to reach our generous benefits system'. Indeed, in the warning words of the *Mail on Sunday*, in March 2001, 'Asylum seekers are a threat to our future'. More recently, in May 2004, a British National Party election leaflet fulminated against a 'tidal wave' which was causing Britain 'to explode'. Certainly, in many quarters the anguished cry goes up: 'They exploit our tolerance and generosity. What are we going to do about that?' To meet queries and demands such as those just referred to will tax the straightforwardness and objectivity of any government, particularly if there is widespread incredulity of the sort voiced by the *Daily Express* in May 2004. 'There is no need', they claim,

> for the NAO (National Audit Office) to tell us that the government's figures on asylum seekers are incomplete and 'materially' misleading. Every citizen knows there has been a cover-up. We can no longer believe anything the government says and we have no faith in its figures.

What was Whitehall doing about the illegal 'Army of Scroungers'? The issue was taken up firmly but rather late in the day by a government which pointed out that asylum claimants were not, in fact, illegal entrants. Under the terms of the 1951 Refugee Convention, they had a right to claim asylum and a state had a responsibility to admit them and to judge the validity of their claim. As for 'sponging' or 'scrounging', the asylum seeker was not allowed to claim mainstream welfare benefits. Only those eventually classified as refugees would receive support in the shape of basic food and shelter. There were in 2004 something like 80,000 asylum seekers 'on benefit' compared with 15.5 million Britons. Indeed, the benefit that they received was less generous than they might have received in Ireland, Belgium or Denmark. It seems doubtful whether coming to the UK to enjoy its welfare benefits has ever been much of a 'pull' factor.

Then what of the *Mail on Sunday*'s fear of the threat to our future? Was our social fabric and economic prosperity being imperilled? A Home Office calculation still broadcast widely is that in general the incomers contribute more to the British economy in taxes and national insurance than they take out, perhaps 10 per cent more. The UK takes only about 2 per cent of the world's refugees in any case. They are hardly a drain on our resources, it is stated, if the asylum system costs a mere 0.425 per cent of government expenditure. Quite slowly, resettlement and integration policies are helping vocationally qualified asylum seekers, perhaps one in three, find employment in the National Health Service which has currently 80,000 vacancies.

As for the 'tidal wave', media sources are at last beginning to dispel this fallacy by printing the frequent statistics showing the prominent fall in applications, which are 50 per cent lower in 2004 than in 2003. Only one in five appeals is allowed and claim failures and removals

Table 3.1 Asylum applications submitted in Britain 1990–8

1990–1	1992	1993–4	1995	1996	1997	1998
73,400	34,500	28,000	55,000	37,000	41,500	58,000

have increased markedly. However, although facts and figures noised abroad officially may reduce alienation and misinformation, the trend towards tougher measures and cutting away at asylum needs is leading to much anxiety in liberal quarters. Could there be any truth in the charge by some critics that 'Whitehall is trying to stop them coming here whether they're genuine or not'?

Uninformed perspectives in press articles and readers' letters are, unfortunately, to be expected. More unhelpful to encouraging objectivity is the evidence of negative perspectives that the rising generation appear to hold. They will have to live in an increasingly multicultural nation. It was in June 2003 that a MORI opinion poll of 18–21 year olds was commissioned by Amnesty International and the Refugee Council. Among their findings were these:

- 48 per cent of young people believe that few asylum seekers in the UK are genuine.
- 58 per cent believe asylum seekers and refugees do not make a positive contribution to the UK social and economic well-being.
- 23 per cent believe that the UK should not offer a safe haven to people fleeing persecution or war.
- 51 per cent believe that asylum seekers in the UK should enjoy the same right to liberty, work and education as other British citizens.

The degree of compatibility among these beliefs is interesting to think about. It seems to point to confusion, to a diet of unfair media coverage and to a lack of informed debate.

Facts and figures

Figures from Home Office Statistical Bulletins and Refugee Council enumeration show that it was in the 1990s that substantial numbers of people were claiming asylum in Britain (see Table 3.1).

As the new century dawned, by 2000 the applicant numbers were levelling out. The main trends reported by the Refugee Council in August 2004 are visible and largely indisputable:

- In 2003, applications for asylum fell by 41 per cent to 49,405.
- The UK experienced the greatest proportionate fall in asylum applications of the major recipient European countries: there were increases for France and Italy. The UK ranks in the middle of EU countries in terms of applications received per 1,000 of population.
- Applications in September 2003 were 4,270, that is, 51 per cent lower than applications in October 2002. The level of applications has continued to fall to around 8,000 in the latest quarter (April to June 2004). Most asylum applicants were from Congo, Sudan, Somalia, Iraq, Afghanistan, Zimbabwe, Sri Lanka and Iran, with three out of four fleeing from scenes of violent conflict or grave human rights violations or both.
- The number of cases currently awaiting initial decision in December 2004 was 9,800, the lowest number for a decade.
- In 2003 there was a record number of appeals where 20 per cent were allowed and 78 per cent refused.
- Again in 2003, an estimated 28 per cent of applications resulted in grants of asylum and of temporary 'exceptional leave to remain' pending the hearing of appeals.
- Asylum removals were 21 per cent higher in 2003 than in 2002 and were 13,005. A large number of failed asylum seekers, 17,895, were removed in 2003, some 29 per cent more than in 2002.

These figures raise questions. Do more claims represent more abuse of the asylum system? Do fewer claims reflect greater global stability? Is it so that fewer claims demonstrate that government controls and restrictive policies are beginning to bite? Moreover, whatever some of the questions, statistics such as these are unwelcome to those critics who see numerical targets as inhumane and contrary to the 1951 Geneva Convention which places upon governments an unequivocal duty to take in all who arrive fleeing from persecution. It was Amnesty International's belief in February 2004 that 'the Home Office continues to focus on getting numbers down, when it should concentrate on getting decisions right'.

Asylum applicants: procedures on arrival

- On entry, prompt applications should go to the Immigration and Nationality Directorate (IND) of the Home Office.
- First screening establishes identity and nationality together with fingerprinting and filming.

- Induction interviews have a dual role – exploration of personal claim via oral and written evidence and explanation of claimant's rights and responsibilities.
- Case workers, trained to act in accordance with the 1951 Convention and with the European Convention on Human Rights, scrutinise each case. Decisions are given through interpreters and in writing.
- Three outcomes are possible: (1) Recognition as a refugee under 1951 Convention terms and so a grant of UK asylum; (2) asylum refused but humanitarian protection or discretionary leave for a limited period is granted since it would be inadvisable or impossible to return to the native land; (3) asylum, protection and discretionary leave refused with a right to appeal.
- Refugee status, if recognised, confers indefinite leave to enter or remain in the UK. Family reunion and the building of a new life are encouraged.
- Refugee status, if not recognised, leads to refusal of asylum and an expectation that they must leave the UK. If they do not do so, they may be detained and deported but only if their personal health and their safety in the country receiving them are assured. Details of appeal process and information about legal representation are given.
- Asylum seekers can ask to be returned to their original country at any time during their claim under an Assisted Return Programme.
- A National Asylum Support Service (NASS) helps any claimants unable to support themselves during their period of claim. Subsistence payments and accommodation are provided. Claimants, though, are to remain in designated accommodation.
- Resettlement and integration within a community is the desirable goal for all recognised refugees. They will have full access to housing, education, employment and medical treatment. Much depends upon individual initiative, outside help from voluntary agencies and a measure of fortunate circumstances in a locality. Integration programmes are being devised all the time by the Home Office and by local authority and other regional bodies.
- Dispersal of claimants is resorted to by the government, which believes that each region in the land should be expected to take its fair share of these people. It is felt that London and the Southeast is overloaded and that other areas should develop a suitable infrastructure of assistance with the aid of local authority and voluntary groups. The National Asylum Support Service is to coordinate general provision of housing, schooling and medical

care and also act as a liaison point for the case worker groups helping individual claimants. Clearly the government realises the urgency of settling and reassuring bewildered claimants, who were often being sent to unfamiliar locations with their own social and economic problems.

Process, procedures and reform

The last ten years have seen much volatility in the number of asylum seekers, a welter of debate, at least five radical rafts of legislation, and an enormity of make do and mend initiatives to cope with problems. Given a downward spiral of claimant numbers, and, understandably, a need, often expressed stridently, to view and review trends and implications, there is on all sides in contemporary Britain a move to reform procedures.

Reform? 'Not before time', most critics would say. Over at least a decade, the UK has been slow to respond to the challenge of flooding immigration. Policies and procedures have been implemented weakly. The surging figures from year to year reflect crises in Yugoslavia, Somalia, Iraq and Afghanistan. Government response has been largely reactive and haphazard and slow to join up in coordinated fashion with the willingness and experience of local authorities and a diverse voluntary sector.

A detailed set of suggestions appeared in June 2004 from a group of eleven NGOs designed to make public suggestions for improving the asylum system. With the title *Refugees: Renewing the Vision*, this was a collection of recommendations from a group of voluntary organisations, among them Amnesty International, the Refugee Council, Oxfam, the Immigration Advisory Service, Refugee Action, and the Scottish Refugee Council, all of them much experienced in intensive work with asylum seekers (Refugee Council, 2004). The collection certainly represents their concern at what they see as inadequacies in the present system. Six points, they feel, need addressing urgently.

In the first place, the procedures in handling the newcomers must be less adversarial, more investigative, not so much attuned to bureaucratic conventions. Some flexibility, more imagination, and less shifting of responsibilities. Second, and in line with a more sympathetic approach (despite the press of numbers), immigration officials must surely acknowledge that asylum seeking is 'gender specific'. Women, children and men have different personal needs as well as characteristics. Children are the most easily hurt if they are handled insensitively. The paper states that each year 20,000 children seek asylum in the

European Union without their parents and suitable carers. Their case, to avoid trauma, calls for prompt reception and continuing consideration. Women, often lamely dependent on an accompanying male claimant, or bundled along on their own, are especially vulnerable, in transit, on arrival, in the interview room, and during the first few months awaiting decision. They will very often find great difficulty in the first phase of resettlement if this is allowed.

Third, the entire induction process needs looking at. Clearer legal access for a claimant is imperative. An applicant must have freely given time to prepare their case, and to gather evidence if an appeal is to be lodged. Interpreters will be there to bridge any language deficit. During the period of waiting on decision, a claimant should be helped to find a job as a means of support. Often, being put in touch with fellow applicants in other localities is a useful form of preliminary support. Better welfare care and benefits are essential. And during the period of marking time while decisions are worked out and promulgated, no applicant whose application is turned down should ever be in fear of precipitate detention and deportation.

Fourth, as a step towards a possible grant of asylum, induction should not tail away into uncertainty but provide some positive introduction into what it is to be ushered into an English community. (The voluntary organisations have long experience of helping asylum seekers find their first footing in Britain, and some help in adjusting to a new world could be given through closer liaison with the government system.) Fifth, and a point to be examined again later in this chapter, resettlement and integration are, of course, the goal of successful asylum seekers but in a very real sense these processes of settling down to a new life begin with arrival on Day One. The recognised refugee should be moved through procedures on a fast track but not insensitively. As the working paper sees it, 'a system of reception, induction and support should be established that enables people to regain control over their lives'. As soon as possible after a decision to grant asylum, those benefiting from that are to have access to opportunities and vocational courses. Protection and enhanced feelings of self-confidence go hand-in-hand. In conclusion, the NGOs affirm, there really is no alternative to a single, simple, effective and transparently fair procedure for all people seeking protection.

Interestingly, in the working paper there is a hint that shedding the political grip over asylum seekers might be a good thing. The authors perhaps had in mind the thoughts of Barbara Roche, a former Home Office minister, who favours a major shift in procedures to make the whole asylum system independent of government from the beginning

(*Guardian*, 15 December 2003, report). This, she believes, would generate confidence in the applicants and a recognition among the general public that the process was as fair as it could be. There ought to be two tribunals, one dealing with immigrant reception and the other with appeals. The Home Office would only sift applications to make sure that none of them was completely unfounded. It was crucial that an applicant had reasonable legal aid and a clear route to appeal if necessary. It is difficult to see most Home Secretaries entertaining proposals which reduce government control.

Asylum seeking: the law and debate

The principal UK laws relating to asylum seekers are these:

1993 Asylum and Immigration Appeals Act – the first attempt to legislate a streamlined approach with firm controls. Visas are introduced. Housing rights are reduced.
1996 Asylum and Immigration Act – provides for fast-tracking of applications, criminalises false entry attempts, brings in more benefit reduction, introduces a 'white list' of 'safe countries'.
1998 Immigration and Asylum Act – brings in a range of sanctions against carriers, provides for detention where necessary, removes benefits rather drastically, arranges for asylum seeker dispersal to provincial 'clusters', increases powers for investigation, search and arrest.
2000 – The National Asylum Support Service (NASS) now responsible for applicant support. Vouchers for seeker adults at 70 per cent of adult benefit and 100 per cent of child benefit to be exchangeable for food and clothes. Ultimately, after wide public criticism, the voucher scheme was withdrawn.

It was in November 2003 that the Home Secretary, David Blunkett, introduced a Bill into the House of Commons. New measures, he said, would be part of a balanced approach to improve the system and clamp down on its abuse. Interestingly, he put all this in the wider context of encouraging a 'legal, managed migration which can make an enormous contribution to our economy and society'.

The Bill was to bring more speed and decisiveness to appeals and removals. Those whose claims fail must go home. 'Working the system' by dishonest and untruthful claimants, sometimes aided by unscrupulous 'advisers', would be stopped. They would face criminal prosecution, as would organised gangs who exact heavy entry payments, lodge false claims, falsify documents, frustrate decisions about appeals or removals, or engage in trafficking for labour exploitation. The Bill was certainly resolute (some would say 'draconian') in requiring power to remove support from families who are able but unwilling to leave the UK when they have exhausted all legal rights to remain and are refusing the offer of a voluntary, paid return home.

A Bill must be laid before Parliament for close discussion as a prelude to its adoption, very likely in modified form, as a parliamentary Act. One can see this Bill was very carefully drafted to take account of the groundswell of public opinion and pressures as well as representations from field workers. There is little doubt that those who would authorise a new parliamentary Act, together with their constituents, needed to be assured that new measures would take even further the emphasis of earlier legislation. Critics, too, especially the media variety, were to be disarmed. To add muscle to the impending Bill, a White Paper was published on 7 February 2002 entitled, surely significantly, *Secure Borders, Safe Haven: Integration with Diversity in Modern Britain.* A key provision of both White Paper and Bill was couched in sterling terms:

> [to] strengthen the integrity of our borders by ensuring that our immigration controls are sufficiently robust to exclude those who are an immigration or security risk, but to be efficient, flexible and responsive so as to speed the entry of the many people who are coming here legitimately.

An important element in the reforming scheme was for tighter collaboration between European governments. Criteria for minimum standards, recognition of claimants' qualifications, rights and benefits would do much to reduce the waiting spells of 'refugees in orbit'. Pinning down states' exact responsibilities was to knock away the possibility of claimants searching for the cheapest and less carefully guarded routes across the English Channel. Together, immigration services in a number of countries would fight the smuggling of immigrants with ever more vigilant searches and inspection of ship cargoes and lorry freight. Any possible import of terrorists would be scrutinised by security services. In Britain the Anti-Terrorism, Crime and Security Act 2001 was to provide authorisation for the surveillance and detention of suspected terrorist agents.

No proposed Bill can avoid being put through hoops by a House of Commons Select Committee. In this case the Home Affairs Select Committee was anxious about proposals for thinning down appeal procedures, for removing at short notice any unsuccessful claimant, and for reducing adjudication safeguards and legal aid. It was clear that certain provisions in the Bill were there because of quite understandable worries about security. Even so, the suggestions for the introduction of 'smart cards', for the electronic tagging of asylum seekers, for segregation, if not in main jails, then in forty ring-fenced 'soft prison' detention centres, all these seemed to some committee members to be at variance with the Geneva spirit and letter. Outside the Commons there were, in fact, protester placards declaring 'Detaining refugees is persecution'.

At last the Bill became law in July 2004, as the Asylum and Immigration Treatment of Claimants Act 2004. Its provisions are now the operative ones. Though most of the reform suggestions previously formulated in the Bill were adopted, they did little to diminish flurries of indignation across the country. Heading into a storm of criticism, David Blunkett, the Home Secretary, let it be known that although the new measures were 'as tough as old boots' he was not 'anti-immigration' but he was determined to improve the asylum system drastically. Some newspapers were more articulate and constructive in their arguments than others and in common with television and radio interviews tended to highlight similar points of concern. Indeed, it could be said that the asylum seeker problem was now earning 'prime time' attention in detail. The Refugee Council was able to contribute a wealth of recommendations from years of intensive case work. New appeal procedures were questioned by many. Why was it desirable now to abolish a two-tier appeals system and replace it with a single-tier tribunal called the Asylum and Immigration Tribunal (AIT)? Was it fair to make a further recourse to the High Court more difficult, with less time for a properly marshalled case and certainly one that was not automatic? Even the Lord Chief Justice had his doubts about that.

Entering the UK without valid documents was now to be a criminal offence. Even the loss or defacing of such documents put an entrant in danger of imprisonment. Was this not, in effect, punishment of a refugee for behaving like a refugee? Over the last fifty years, many thousands of refugees have fled their homes with the barest of necessities, unable to get valid documentation from an authority from whose persecution they are escaping. It is likely that women, in particular, may not have access to or own their own travel or identity papers.

The Act of 2004 will be there in the statute book firmly enough, but its tenor will be deplored by many who have to wrestle with the unforeseen and the incalculable, factors which make for problematic dealings with inarticulate and apprehensive seekers after a safe and ordered existence. No doubt there will be continued anxiety on all sides that what appears to government to be a priority for deterrence will short-change claimants financially, legally and politically.

At the end of the day: resettlement and integration

A recent study (Kushner and Knox 2001: 15–16) considers the issue of how successfully asylum seekers and refugees adapt to life in another country. A chain-like personal cycle of adaptation generally begins with feelings of confusion and disorientation on arrival, followed often by disillusion mixed with relief at escape, as expectations are seldom met. Emotional anxieties stemming from alienation, loss and isolation are commensurate with projection into another world of uncertainty where others, if they are able to acknowledge these visible feelings, may help or clumsily step aside. The process of adaptation or acculturation may take years to achieve and will vary with age, gender, language and ethnicity and often whether the would-be settler is alone or with family. How is resettlement success measured? This is an impossible question to ask of a refugee. Governments probably rate success in terms of numbers seeking and receiving asylum. A voluntary organisation may regard a reduction in individual and group demands as a pointer to secure resettlement. A local authority is grateful that at last accommodation and employment needs appear to have been met reasonably by those now clearly 'settling in'. A critical issue remains. When, from the refugee's own point of view, do self-sufficiency factors such as locale, living standards, access to amenities and unqualified acceptance by others constitute a bridge crossed with confidence and security? The refugee no longer stumbles through the dark. There can be no need and no incentive 'to return'.

An important follow-on process in rehabilitating asylum seekers is what is known as integration. Two objectives for helping these people achieve a tolerable quality of life, and a move towards reaching fuller potential, have been made dynamic in devoted casework by a number of voluntary associations. A contemporary emphasis, now in government circles and among local authorities, is to devise appropriate strategies to realise, it has been said, a significant difference in refugee lives and in the communities in which they live.

The Refugee Council published in May 2004 a draft document for consultation with the Home Office, voluntary bodies and community sector organisations (Refugee Council, 'Agenda for Integration', May 2004). A reading of this gives an excellent overview of the principles, policies and practical methods that can and should be used to grasp the challenges of working with asylum seekers. An outline of the proposed strategies begins with a forthright statement: 'Integration is a term that can evoke different associations but actually is a two-way process, which places demands on both the receiving society and on the refugee. As such, integration is not assimilation.' This would seem to require of the refugee a willingness to adapt to a host society's lifestyle without sacrificing his own cultural identity. Understandably, such adaptation will be far from easy. On the other hand, a host society, if it is to advance any integration, must be ready to accept refugees as equals, and not as marginalised adherents to a community. No time is to be lost in bringing fresh approaches into effect, for delay prompts exclusion, demoralisation and loss of self-confidence and skills.

A multi-faceted, generously resourced and coordinated programme is reckoned to bestow a sense of belonging and membership in an inclusive, welcoming community. The major routes to integration will be channelled through mainstream schools and colleges, vocational guidance and vocational training. Access, retention, achievement and progress are often rehearsed in heady rhetoric yet they are frequently unrealisable – the opportunities are not there for grasping. The 'buzzwords' in this and other documents, for instance, networks, connections, job creation schemes, regional consortia, monitoring criteria, need lacing together so that asylum seekers appreciate their significance as helping hands.

An ongoing concern among local authorities is to make certain that accommodation is secure, safe and sustainable for those who are dispersed to the provinces. At present, it is estimated that two thirds of asylum seekers are living with relatives, friends or others nearby. No effort should be spared to provide something that the seeker after asylum may call 'home'. Nor should it be overlooked that many of those who have fled have suffered trauma in the homeland, during transit, and often as a result of stress coping with a new environment. This situation must lead to Primary Care Trusts and specialist clinics developing schemes of comprehensive health assessment and continued care.

Provisions and programmes such as those outlined above may strike many readers as good in theory but needing rapid translation into 'best practice'. Fortunately, there is now every sign that Whitehall and local authorities will be working methodically and with a new momentum to implement plans.

Out in the shires

Meanwhile, out in the provinces there are a number of interesting initiatives to resettle and integrate asylum seekers. Dispersal out of London and the crowded Southeast seemed the only feasible way of dealing effectively and humanely with a flow of asylum seekers. As far as one can see, responses in the regions are diverse and complex. There are those field workers who describe happenings optimistically; others resort to detailed criticism and sometimes invective. For many of the last group, 'it's the English that are the problem!'

Readers will have to judge for themselves the validity of principle and the effectiveness of practice, and may do so either through the Refugee Council in London or the Information Centre about Asylum and Refugees in the UK (ICAR), recently established at Kings College, London. The ICAR website (www.icar.org.uk) is invaluable, enabling the 'visitor' to the site to access a wealth of information about a particular area of Britain, its historical and contemporary experience of asylum seekers and its approach to their resettlement. This project is still in development and only a selected number of areas are as yet available. Nevertheless, what is available affords a remarkable picture of challenge and response. Sheffield, for instance, a city of half a million, has people from sixty-three nations living there. This represents a mingling of sixty-three distinctive cultures. Those born outside the European Union in 2001 were 6 per cent of the city's residents. And in some Sheffield wards one in three was non-native born. Those looking for sanctuary in Sheffield make up three groups. There are the newly-arrived 'dispersals', directed by government. There are, ever since 1939, Belgians, Poles, Czechs, Germans, Chileans, Ugandans, Sri Lankans, Vietnamese – asylum seekers or refugees from earlier political upheavals abroad and now settled in their own mini-communities. Then, there are the asylum seekers coming in from other parts of Britain to join relatives and friends in the city. An estimated 6,000 school students work in sixty different languages. Somehow the mixture and the problems are being addressed by a great assortment of voluntary organisations working in partnership as a joined-up service. There is on offer and on trial a jigsaw of enterprises focusing on housing, health, employment, schooling and college enrolment. There are programmes and projects, strategy groups and 'lifelines'. Other places, like Southampton and Leicester, for example, have similar problems and they are only half the size of Sheffield. Again, there are some sixty-three cultures close upon one another. Leicester, indeed, is England's top of the league microcosm, with one in five of the townsfolk born outside the UK.

The invisibles

Optimism and pessimism are the mood moments of most who work alongside asylum seekers. From time to time in many localities there is despair as to how best to save the newcomers from exploitation. This is a nefarious form of integration that nobody can tolerate. Over perhaps two decades, a network has sprung up of bogus 'advisors', fraudulent landlords and plainly dishonest agents and entrepreneurs touting job opportunities. They know all the loopholes in their search for ready-to-pay victims. With jobs there are no questions asked in 'Job Street'. Nor are there work permits, nor ready money agreement, nor rights. An underclass is pinned down by a 'black economy' where the gang master rules. Perhaps 30,000 'illegals' pick early flowers in Cornwall, peas in Lincolnshire, and fruit in Kent. They are the 'invisibles', all too often ignored by the rest of society. Many are from Eastern Europe, Southeast Asia and the impoverished districts of Latin America, sometimes slipping past the immigration net at the ports as 'students' or 'tourists'. They toil for sixteen hours a day for seven days a week and retire to poor housing and extortionate rents. Now and then, disaster strikes, looming large in a day's headlines. The nineteen Chinese picking cockles in Morecambe Bay in the spring of 2004 were said to earn in two months what would have taken them a year in their native land. They paid with their lives. Of course, every effort is made by the authorities to trace the sweated illegality and brutality of what looks like a return to the worst excesses of the early Industrial Revolution.

The visibles and the need for action

They are, of course, highly visible in the streets, those who are looking for a safer life. They have a right not to be ignored. In many respects, perhaps, they are the focus of two opposing pressures, the proud tradition of Britain as a sanctuary and the other belief, that we cannot stand further dilution and diversity. Then, is Britishness so fragile that it is unable to absorb a significant number of 'others'? The point, possibly a dilemma for some people, is well put in a recent study:

> There is now a very grave danger of Britain swallowing whole its own mythologies to the point of hypocrisy: of it becoming a country committed to asylum without the possibility of entry; of a haven for the oppressed without the presence of refugees.
>
> (Kushner and Knox 2001: 417)

There follows a call for action. 'By facing our global responsibilities towards the displaced, we begin the process of changing for the better a world which creates the misery of growing refugee movements.' This question and the others already discussed will be further considered, in a European context, in the following chapter.

4   Asylum seekers in Europe

Facts and debate

Défense d'entrer is the signpost most British motorists have seen as they turn out of one of the Channel ferry terminals and encounter one-way streets and roadworks. There are people today who declare that such signs should be erected permanently at the gates of Fortress Europe. This makes the point in very direct terms that those who are not We Europeans are not welcome. Legal restrictions, prejudice and waning liberalism are increasingly shutting those gates. The problem of so many seeking entry to the continent is regarded, so we are told, as a 'hot button issue' in every single European country. Contemporary Europe is a most confused place.

This chapter follows on from a study of Britain's dealings with seekers after asylum and attempts to consider how Europe in general and the European Union's (EU) twenty-five members cope with something so demanding. The chapter design is threefold – figures, facts and debate. First, a survey of statistics, then a broad factual outline of processes and procedures from reception to integration, and finally a balanced look at a debate which grows anguished and strident.

The figures below (Tables 4.1, 4.2 and 4.3) have been culled from sources published by UNHCR in Geneva, by the Refugee Council in London and, also in London, by the European Council for Refugees and Exiles (ECRE). (The helpfulness of these source providers is most

Table 4.1 Asylum applications submitted in the EU 1990–2002

1990	1991	1992	1993	1994	1995	1996
400,315	509,493	675,455	516,398	309,722	274,951	233,415
1997	1998	1999	2000	2001	2002	2003
251,762	311,408	396,737	391,275	388,372	381,623	309,330

Source: UNHCR Statistical Yearbook 2001

Table 4.2 Asylum requests to European Union countries in 2003, 1999–2001

Country	No.	Country	No.
United Kingdom	61,050	Ireland	7,900
France	51,360	Italy	*7,280
Germany	50,450	Spain	5,770
Austria	32,340	Denmark	4,560
Sweden	31,360	Finland	3,060
Belgium	16,940	Luxembourg	1,550
Netherlands	13,400	Portugal	110
Greece	8,180		

Source: UNHCR Asylum applications 2000–2002, Table 8

* 2002 data

gratefully acknowledged.) One or two points about the statistics need stating. In the first place, as was pointed out earlier, the figures quoted should be understood as provisional and as approximations given the difficulties of Europe-wide collection. Second, and in consequence, it is never easy to obtain up-to-the-minute numbers. Third, and most usefully, readers can readily examine figures and trends by accessing the source websites (these are listed at the back of this book).

It is frequently assumed that asylum applications increase year on year in Europe. These figures show that this is not the case. Between 1988 and 1992 (the peak year), numbers rose from 210,900 to 675,455. In the early 1990s, the increasing numbers had much to do with Balkan wars and with increased repressive measures in Turkey and Romania. In the later 1990s, people were flooding out of Afghanistan, Somalia and Rwanda and eventually from Iraq.

The oscillation in these figures demonstrates the ebb and flow of conflict situations and, perhaps, in the case of Turkey, Iran and China, apprehensions on the part of those intending to leave their native land. It is interesting to compare the ratio of applicants to the population of the host countries: for instance, in 2003, in Austria the ratio was 3.9, in Norway 3.5, Sweden 3.5, in Switzerland 2.9, Belgium 1.9, the UK 1.0 and in Germany 0.9. In 2002, the UK received most asylum applicants, totalling 110,700 and then falling by 41 per cent to 49,405 (Source: Refugee Council, *In Exile*, September 2004, issue 33). Annual asylum seeker statistics have varied, altering these ratios.

Discussion of asylum seeker problems tends to focus not so much on raw figures as on what are thought to be statistical trends. The Refugee Council's estimate in the first quarter of 2004, that Europe was already accommodating 4,268,000 asylum seekers and refugees, was in some quarters presented as a tidal wave of immense proportions and one

Table 4.3 Origin of asylum applicants arriving in the EU

Country	1999	Country	2000	Country	2001
Yugoslavia, FR	82,726	Iraq	38,852	Iraq	41,249
Iraq	25,328	Yugoslavia, FR	36,564	Afghanistan	37,429
Turkey	17,628	Afghanistan	31,692	Turkey	27,312
Afghanistan	16,778	Turkey	25,472	Yugoslavia, FR	22,992
Somalia	12,292	Iran	20,730	Russian Fed.	12,792
Iran	11,315	China	12,906	Iran	11,999
China	10,506	Sri Lanka	11,615	Sri Lanka	9,963
Russian Fed.	10,470	Russian Fed.	11,577	Somalia	9,929
Sri Lanka	9,857	Bosnia	9,401	Algeria	8,908
Romania	7,811	Herzegovina	n.a.	Bosnia	8,778
		Somalia	9,347	Herzegovina	n.a.

Source: Population Data Unit, UNHCR, Geneva

that was likely to grow even higher. In fact, the number of asylum applications has declined from a peak of almost 700,000 in 1992 and subsequently went lower after 1995 to 309,000 in 2003. Recently, in March 2004, Ruud Lubbers, the UN's High Commissioner for Refugees, confirmed that applicant numbers are continuing to drop sharply. In that case, he says, 'there is no need to focus so single-mindedly on reducing standards [of refugee protection] and trying to deter or deny protection to as many people as possible'.

The general direction of statistical trends, not unexpectedly, is showing a steadying of application numbers from Yugoslavia, Afghanistan, and Iraq, in particular, as some sort of very fragile stability takes root there under foreign assistance or guard. Applications from Somalia and Congo have hardly lessened, reflecting the fratricide and famine that persist. Quite evident altogether is a marked falling away of applications accepted by European Union states as their welcome cools and contra-regulations begin to bite. Belgium, Denmark, the Netherlands and, to some extent, Germany, all of whom have good records as host states, have during the last two years shown an edge to their willingness to accept asylum seekers. Ireland, Spain, Switzerland and Sweden have held their positions as acceptors, despite much querulous publicity, though here, too, preliminary scrutiny and eventual admission procedures are more stringent than hitherto.

Facts: reception and procedures in general

Figures apart, it is worthwhile taking a general look at the shape of Europe's dealing with asylum seekers as it has developed during the last few years and prior to more recent attempts to 'harmonise' procedures. (This task will be described in detail later in the chapter.) The scenario in which European states have devised policies to deal with asylum seeking has been described in Home Office Research Study 259 of June 2003. In brief and in outline, the study describes developments in what might be termed six phases:

Phase 1 – the early and mid-1970s. A time of increasing global mobility shadowed by an incident of crisis in the developing world, and so Europe encouraged immigration of non-Europeans to meet labour shortages while it hosted refugee flows from Vietnam. As the number of third country nationals grew, entry conditions began to be tightened.

Phase 2 – the 1980s saw the collapse of the Soviet Bloc and a massive exodus, part-permanent, part-temporary, from East to West as physical transit became easier and political barriers relaxed. Germany, facing substantial immigration, hardened its stance.

Phase 3 – the earlier 1990s, an era when European states were attempting to distinguish immigrants responding to a rising economic dynamic from those coming in as products of clandestine entry and trafficking. There were twin modes of action: expansion and restriction, leading inevitably to growing tension.

Phase 4 – the later 1990s. Treaties such as Maastricht 1993 and Amsterdam 1997 ushered in supranational efforts when states' policies started to converge in a process they termed 'harmonisation'. Pressures from the public sector and the media were now querying the existence of immigrant 'threat' and the feasibility of 'integration'.

Phase 5 – around 2000, clear dividing lines in policy-driven action in regard to (a) pre-entry containment (resort to visas, fining of illegal carriers, stringent checking); and (b) in-country deterrence (fast-tracking procedures, limited appeal possibilities, detention, restricted access to work and social assistance benefit). Cutting across this, and briefly, was the outflow of short-term refugees from 'safe havens' created by coalition and NATO forces during the first Gulf War and in the Former Republic of Yugoslavia.

Phase 6 – the contemporary scene – tensions, recrimination and questioning are elements in a broader debate about the extent to which Europe, notably the enlarging European Union, can feasibly honour obligations towards refugees and asylum seekers. Greece, Spain, Austria, Belgium and Britain are also tightening state support and work access for asylum applicants. European standards of reception, classification and rights to appeal are diminishing. Do the old conventions and protocols call for redrawing? In some countries (Britain is one of them) receptor policies are positive, practical and welcoming. Otherwise, liberals and human rights activists deplore wide lack of understanding in the press and among wide sections of the public and harsher tendencies towards harsh governmental reaction. They see some governments – Belgium, the Netherlands, France, Austria – being more worried about immigration numbers than the quality of admission practice.

All European countries find themselves coping with the dilemma of reconciling their humanitarian duty to protect those who seek refuge with the practical task of distinguishing valid entrants from the invalid. Three aspects of this, particularly, have made for difficulty in handling and raise controversy, namely, entry documentation, transit between homeland and proposed haven, and illegal trafficking.

Entry documents such as a visa with photograph have been a standard requirement, despite the advice of UNHCR that those fleeing persecution or violence should not be forced into this situation; moreover, common sense suggests that few of these unfortunate people will be able to approach a diplomatic mission back home asking for travel facilities. Predictably, European unrelenting insistence is spawning a network of agents and phantom companies who will forge a bogus visa for an extortionate charge. Transit arrangements similarly lead to a cat-and-mouse game. Large numbers of desperate people attempt illicit Channel crossings, chancing it through the tunnel or in the confines of a lorry. Trafficking is another response to harsh anti-immigration policies. Germany estimates that half its asylum seekers are smuggled over the frontiers and the Netherlands believes seven out of ten travel that route. A UN protocol, ratified by forty states in 2002, attempts to fasten on to illegality by encouraging very careful scrutiny at entry points, with every consideration given to those who genuinely flee persecution albeit at a horrendous cost.

The task of classification

Asylum seekers who crowd points of entry are classified on sight, as it were, with a more careful investigation to follow. There is every sign these days that the strict and simple crucial definitions of the 1951 Convention and the 1967 Protocol are being interpreted loosely and inconsistently. Some states have adopted only a partial understanding, for instance, by excluding refugees persecuted by non-state agents. To determine whether there is a 'well-founded fear' of persecution there must be a reliance on a witness's oral evidence, and it is clearly not easy to lay the lines of how this process should be carried out. Generally, reception procedures have used a threefold classification:

- Convention Recognised Status – confers permanent or indefinite leave to remain together with entitlement to welfare standards at least comparable to those enjoyed by citizens and resident aliens. These requirements are comprehensive since 2003 to ensure that reading of the Convention is not restrictive.
- Complementary Protection – this ought to be offered to those who flee civil strife or aggression or genocide. The principle of non-refoulement is critical. Unfortunately, this protection system is neither consistent nor complete. Some states award referrals the same rights as Convention Refugees, other states give them secondary status with fewer, non-permanent rights. A number of states strain to show tolerance or provision of any rights and aim at deportation of those they term 'benefit tourists'.
- Temporary Protection – this may be offered on terms approved by UNHCR and indicates that the applicant would find return to the homeland too dangerous. Britain suggested in May 2003 the creation of 'asylum zones' or 'protection zones' outside the EU where claims would be screened and refugees housed until their homeland circumstances were judged more secure. A majority of EU members turned down the proposal to begin with, but in June 2003 they reluctantly agreed to a pilot scheme in East Africa in 2004.

A term aborting everything an applicant is seeking is that of 'manifestly unfounded'. An increasing number of states have resorted to this label since 1952 and on rather hazy grounds. A consequence is uncertainty, even detention, while a case is under investigation. Apart from delay, a worse outcome is for the case to be put on 'fast-track' where documentation or other evidence of the applicant's plight is lacking or where the homeland is considered to be unsafe for return. Especially for those suffering from the trauma of a forced eviction, this can be a harrowing situation, particularly if they are separated from their families and also if legal safeguards may be at risk. Possibly with some overworked immigration officials employing the term, there may be more confusion than 'alien phobia'. As for detention, this is often a consequence of doubts raised on arrival, or because investigatory procedures have been delayed or as a prelude to deportation. The UK, for instance, detains most immigrants for longer and with less judicial supervision than any other EU state. In the eyes of UNHCR, detention is a punitive action and should only be used if an applicant is liable to be prosecuted for a serious non-political offence. It would also be permissible in the case of repeated and unjustified unreadiness to cooperate with the authorities, and certainly where an applicant will not comply with a valid deportation order.

The right to stay and work

This is an issue that has provoked much debate in governmental circles across Europe with the result that there is gross unevenness in policies. France, Italy, Spain and Denmark do not allow applicants to find jobs while their status is being confirmed and they have strict rules as to residence-and-work permits. Germany is worried about adding to the labour force when there is significant unemployment. In Britain there has been a shift in an official preference for applicants to wait and see how their status is determined before they find work. Generally, there and elsewhere in Europe, it would seem sensible to allow access to the job market, for many asylum seekers are skilled people, keen to find security and a wage, ready to fill many of the hundreds of thousands of vacancies in catering, construction and transport. Permission to work would be a two-way benefit, helping individuals integrate into the community and reducing the costs to the exchequer of minimum welfare payment.

The whole picture is made complex by the ramifications of a hidden, 'black' economy. Far too many asylum seekers are tangled into a nefarious web of illegal employment, 'gang masters' and exploiters. Britain has a double-edged problem here in attempting to distinguish the genuinely persecuted from the opportunistic. Although in 2003–4 there has been a 41 per cent fall in asylum applications, the numbers of those knocking on the door from Eastern Europe is slow to slacken. A European scheme of 'managed migration' set up in the spring of 2004 has as objectives both a humanitarian sieving of applicants and a rigorous capping on numbers.

Safe third countries

Much heat has been expended on this issue. Europe's governments have framed earnest questions. Could not applicant numbers be sensibly and materially reduced if such people were returned to the country through which they had passed, or where they had lived, if that country – an asylum, in fact – were deemed appropriate and safe? Is it not possible to go further and draw up, as Britain has done, a 'white list' of countries which are stable, peaceful and not unwelcoming to entrants, from which no application to seek asylum in the European Union states is deemed permissible? There have been criticisms from UNHCR and Amnesty International. They are anxious that information about the 'safe' countries might be incomplete, vague, even questionable. In that case, short of a guarantee of dependable admission and determination procedures there, a return might well be hazardous.

Integration

For the asylum seeker and refugee, the difficulties are only just beginning when asylum is granted. The obligation on receiving countries to grant fair treatment on acceptance in respect of housing and employment and welfare is widely side-stepped. There has been little or no consensus in Europe about helping those who are accorded 'security of tenure' to cope with problems of language, family reunion, accommodation, health care and education, in other words, the business of resettlement and putting down some sort of roots in a welcoming community while retaining some sense of personal and cultural identity. Sweden, Ireland, Finland and Britain have introduced a range of carefully designed programmes to address the problems of people-in-transit. More often than not, there are no specific arrangements.

Things as they ought to be: the beginnings of reform

In face of an international problem, European procedures have grown ever more unpredictable and ungoverned. Policies and procedures became encumbered with bureaucratic tardiness, lack of consistency and tolerance. Plain understanding fell away, the prey of fallacies about numbers. Inevitable confusion surrounded the latest human crisis, there was indecision about priorities, and even the Great Threat represented by terrorist outrage. Reform was absolutely necessary, provided all agreed its shape and timing and, above all, its humanitarian imperatives. A pan-European master scheme would take over from an intergovernmental 'contact-and-get-by' piecemeal approach. Some notable steps in the crafting of common policies have been these:

*   January 1951 – the UN's Geneva Convention codifies states' obligations towards refugees who are the victims of European events.
*   January 1967 – a UN Protocol extends protection to all refugees irrespective of date and origin.
*   June 1990 – the Schengen Treaty and Convention make for the ending of internal border controls and for unimpeded travel

throughout Europe. (Only the United Kingdom and Ireland do not ratify.) Yet, external border controls continue to regulate immigration.

- June 1990 – the Dublin Convention lays down the responsibility of states to examine asylum requests and to coordinate the way they do it.
- February 1992 – the Maastricht Treaty sets out to promote a Europe-wide framework for asylum policy and legislation.
- June 1997 – the Amsterdam Treaty strengthens joint action on asylum seeker issues via 'action plans' and 'working groups'. Detailed minimum standards are formulated in respect of reception, classification, procedures and (at least) temporary protection. For the first time, when the treaty really got under way in early 1999, it would be possible to talk meaningfully of a European Asylum Policy. The term 'burden sharing' was prominent in ensuing governmental discussions.
- October 1999 – the Tampere Conclusion is a firm consensus as to policy objectives and it frames directives on basic procedures. There are to be guarantees grounded in full application of the 1951 Convention and on 'absolute respect for the right to claim asylum'.
- 1999–2003 – Successive directives from the European Commission govern minimum protection standards. States, though, are given the opportunity to opt out of some of these in particular circumstances. There are measures to cope with illegal immigration.
- April 2003 – an accession treaty is to enlarge the European Union. Ten states wanting to be full EU members in May 2004 ratify the treaty. They will move into the evolving structure of Europe's asylum seeker policy and action.
- March–April 2004 – the Council of the European Union approves the text of directives fine-tuning refugee definition, degrees of protection awarded, and appeal rights.

Things as they ought to be: reassessment and debate

Despite the steps taken by European Union members and, certainly, outside the heady rhetoric of governments proclaiming their humanitarian intentions towards hapless seekers after refuge, both the pace and the directions of reform have increasingly lacked a uniform drive. The early readiness to harbour those who were persecuted and to go further in welcoming an eclectic mix of cultures has waned over the last decade, as most governments have dug in heels partly in response to media and electoral pressures. Preparedness to collaborate with NGOs was a prominent feature of improved policy-making, to begin with, in Scandinavia, the Netherlands, Britain and Ireland, yet their resolution began to erode as public awareness, orchestrated by the media, put up the notion of the threat from the Legions of the Unwanted. It is probably only the determination of liberal campaigners in a number of countries that has forced governments to come together to reassess the pace and the directions so clearly going askew. Minimum standards must go further than relying upon a lowest common denominator.

The European Council on Refugees and Exiles (ECRE), together with the Refugee Council in London, lost no time, already in May 1994, in bringing into prominence an array of questions designed to pinpoint re-examination of policies. Clearly, those seeking asylum were being short served. Would European states go on making policy secretly and outside democratic structures? Were they not in some ways capitulating to the extreme right for short-term electoral reasons? Could they not do far more to ensure fair treatment and common legal action for refugees? Was it so that some governments would be able to continue opting out of certain obligations on the grounds of cost, inconvenience and 'realpolitik'? Were we all unable to use our energies and creativity to construct a positive, comprehensive and watertight refugee policy?

It is ECRE once more in the forefront of reassessment of policy and practice. Time has moved on and the reform agenda of October 1999 which was loudly trumpeted in Tampere, Finland, is now itself needing scrutiny. The debate is 'on scene'. Reform must be re-formed. Eventually, the partner states involved in policy 'harmonisation' in 1999 decided to convene in Brussels in June 2004, five years after the Tampere meeting. Their deliberations have been evaluated recently in ECRE and summarised in stark terms: BROKEN PROMISES – FORGOTTEN PRINCIPLES (ECRE, June 2004).

At the head of the list is the contextual point that Europe has now enlarged to the extent of twenty-five states, each a different, sovereign entity. If justice is to be done towards the seekers after security, a codex of minimum standards must be drawn up, fairer and more practicable than foregoing ones, and ratified by the twenty-five. It will no longer do for states to rely on a package of procedures and laws that reflect concern with narrow national agendas. The last five years, in ECRE's view, represent 'a missed opportunity' to promote the protection and integration of refugees, rather than deterrence. Minimum standards and safeguards are nowhere near adequate. The concept of the 'safe' third country is an example of flawed thinking, all too often a device for dodging prime responsibility for offering asylum where it can be guaranteed. Moreover, it fails to ensure that no person could even be sent back to possible persecution – non-refoulement was supposed to be a sacred principle. Not only is this principle endangered, there is the halfway house of temporary and subsidiary protection. What sort of protection is it if it places an individual in limbo and, importantly, does little to bring together members of an asylum seeker's family? The crux of how far contemporary Europe guarantees the absolute right to seek asylum, sacrosanct in the 1951 Convention, is the tenuous balancing of humanitarian concern over against the need to secure reliable border control, an aspect of state sovereignty. The last decade has seen huge investment in surveillance, detection and control systems (again, the fear of terrorism is there) and rather less concentration of resources on improved admission procedures. There seems here to be an imbalance whereby the political will to adopt and implement measures to reduce immigration takes precedence over the need for asylum safeguards. Governments frequently claim that their restrictive policies are designed to combat misuse of asylum seeking by unjustified claimants.

The directives that underpin asylum policy are scrutinised by ECRE. Do they offer minimum guarantees to an applicant from which there can be no opt-out even in so-called fast-track procedures? Basically, these should be unimpeded access to a European country, the services of an interpreter and, where possible, impartial counselling, personal and unconditional interviewing, and a clear right of appeal with appropriate legal representation. At a later stage in treating asylum seekers, there still seems, regrettably, a substantial level of freedom in how to receive and accommodate newly arrived applicants. Placements in reception centres, in ECRE's view, must not increase the risks of premature institutionalisation, loss of personal initiative, and aversion to the designated host society. This point begs the question of the extent to which EU measures facilitate the integration of asylum seekers into the societies of member states. There are certainly indications, for instance, in France, Denmark and Greece, that any form of temporary and subsidiary protection lessens the chance of dependable, legal employment and cuts down welfare 'core benefits' to an unrealistic level. Where health care is inadequate, the dangers to applicants and their families, particularly to children, may be life-threatening.

Harmonisation as a form of agreed and shared control is undeniably difficult to shape, especially if there are two dozen partners. Apart from the written-down directives and the buzz of daily communication, there are so-termed High Level Working Groups on Migration and Asylum with the task of preparing EU Action Plans and developing operational proposals to increase members' cooperation and attention to standards in the rulebook. According to some critics, the devil in the detail is too much concentration on 'managing' migration flows through tighter immigration measures and legislation. This may have something to do with the notion, apparently common in some ministries, that relaxing immigration controls would encourage a 'domino effect' of applicants perceiving an easier entry somewhere. No state wants to be involved with the risks of 'harmonising down'. There is almost certainly a wide perception among intending asylum seekers that entry to the northern 'core' of harder-ruling states is difficult compared with the chances of entering the peripheral southern flank of Spain, Italy and Portugal. For the bereft, there is every inducement to go here and there 'asylum shopping'. Associated with this is the tactic of getting a foothold just north of the Mediterranean into legally established resident communities of Somalis, Kurds and Sri Lankans. The usefulness of this conduit is well understood by traffickers and other covert 'movement managers'.

Pre-eminent in the earlier Tampere meeting and now in Brussels is the issue of transparency and democratic control. One question with contemporary salience is the extent to which the new member states will be able to handle the large numbers of applicants. The Dublin Convention of 1990 and its successive addenda rule that the first EU country an asylum seeker enters must be the one to process the application. In most cases these countries will be the very states with the most recent and the thinnest immigration inspection structures and where the business of asylum scrutiny is least sophisticated. It may well happen that some asylum seekers will regard these countries as transit zones, ones which appeal as a 'soft touch'. Apart from this contingency, there is the question of just how careful governments are to hold an adequately open and timely dialogue with NGOs and other public groups. Tampere held this to be a most important channel of communication. The clear potential benefits of addressing asylum at European level need the clearing of a great deal of brushwood blocking understanding and progress – today's information technology can be a powerful 'mutualising' instrument.

A concluding point raised by ECRE and other commentators is that it is rarely straightforward to discern links between policies and outcomes. Similar policies may have different outcomes in various places owing to the influence of domestic political circumstances and law systems, diverse historical and traditional sympathies and perception of human need. What works here may not work there. Indeed, outcomes may not be direct consequences of what is official action in Paris, London or Berlin. Refugees' perceptions, either direct or through hearsay, are quite likely to influence their reaction to what they understand as policies. Will they be welcomed or frozen out? There is also the unpredictability of what might be termed governmental response to a crisis in the developing world which sends streams of desperate people towards civilised sanctuary. Europe in tears will be expected to furnish immediate relief, but will the consequence be a lasting preparedness to hold doors open?

The next round of harmonisation

UNHCR has suggested that the next round of harmonisation discussion and planning offers better prospects for a true European consensus based on agreed high protection standards. New actors, the European Court of Justice and the European Parliament, will become more involved, along with the European Commission, in reliance on majority decisions rather than waiting for unanimity. Two new directions of movement by European states have been outlined by UNHCR. Now there seems more willingness to allocate substantial resources to crisis areas, partly to prevent local conflicts from spinning out of control and certainly to help build the sort of conditions that will see a lessening of a desperate outflow of people. Then, also, there is a promising degree of liaison between receptor states and UNHCR, for example, in the setting up of centralised reception centres where asylum seekers wishing to enter the EU would be processed quickly and efficiently by multi-national teams sharing the task. No state would be burdened with a disproportionate number of refugees. Rejected applicants would be returned carefully and only to countries certified as quite safe by UNHCR.

The UNHCR's High Commissioner, Ruud Lubbers, believes that, at last, European states are placing much more emphasis on the quality of their response to asylum seeking in industrialised countries, while at the same time they are concerned to improve conditions in the countries of refugee origin, so that those who go home are able to stay and fewer will be forced to leave. This is now a time of challenge, to shift from a largely negative approach – closed borders, detention, benefit slashing – to one which focuses on continuing the ancient tradition of welcoming refugees. For Europe and the wider world it is UNHCR which, for half a century, has been the lodestar of those needing sanctuary. The following chapter will tell its story.

5 Globality of concern
The UN and refugees

The public mood was very different as the Second World War drew to a close. It was soft-nosed and embracing in its fellow feeling and deep humanitarian concern. Europe's roads were crowded with hordes of people streaming out of the newly liberated countries so recently occupied by Nazi tyranny. Similarly, in Southeast Asia the plight of the dispossessed and desperate was plain to see. Ready compassion, strong in spirit and ready in provision of relief, marked a general and genuine response to turmoil and suffering. Helping them out and taking them in were the practical goals for a sympathetic effort born of a pragmatic realisation that this was the only thing to do. The infant United Nations, speaking through its General Assembly, commissioned the setting up of an agency to address the huge problem of peoples' displacement. It would be known as the Office of the High Commissioner for Refugees and its function would be humanitarian and social and of an entirely non-political character. Those who were to design the agency and to craft an enabling Convention were given three weeks from 1 January 1951 to realise the enterprise. Very possibly, those who worked on the prototype were energised by a faith that their efforts set up a movement as a transitory feature of a world passing from disastrous conflict to peace. This must have seemed so, given the getting-by-for-now nature of relief organisations deployed to serve soup and comfort in Europe. The United Nations Relief and Rehabilitation Authority (UNRRA) provided 7 million people, among them Arabs evicted from Israel, with temporary housing. The International Refugee Organisation (IRO), a smaller group, resettled more than a million Displaced Persons (DPs) around the world. On a larger scale and still with an expected short-term remit, the new United Nations High Commission for Refugees (UNHCR) would be expected to fill out a three-year stint to 'clear' the refugee crisis and, with solutions in place, thankfully disband.

It is interesting, for a moment, to reflect on what had happened about refugees after the earlier world war of 1914–18. Then, too, mainly within Europe, there had been a wholesale flight of refugees, both from the battlefield and from those violations which are the result of tyrannical neglect and oppression. The League of Nations (the United Nations' ancestor) had hoisted into place a provisional relief organisation and in 1921 put in charge as High Commissioner a Norwegian Arctic explorer, Fridtjof Nansen. Inside a year or two, he performed wonders. His improvisation brought back home half a million prisoners of war from tented camps in revolutionary Russia. His planning and gigantic determination resettled 200,000 White Russian émigrés throughout Europe and across to the United States. His resourcefulness ('difficulties take a little time; the impossible always takes a little longer') set about feeding 10 million starving Ukrainians. Working twelve hours a day, Nansen's ancient car penetrated the border areas of Greece and Turkey and brought resuscitation to 300,000 bewildered farm workers.

Nansen was perhaps the only man able to take on a vast relief operation which would have defeated any League committee. In his case, the job was done, and it demonstrated how a similar job might be done with powerful initiative and long-range viewing. The charisma of this first High Commissioner showed what could be achieved through indomitable self-confidence, a gift for detailed preparation, and a gift, also, for finding the way past governmental prevarication and obstruction. In a decisive manner he side-stepped those who saw themselves as 'realists' and those who were rated as 'arch-conformists', yet without being anything other than understanding and tolerant towards them. Unable to persuade a timid League (they were, after all, unused to firm international collaboration), he rescued refugees in a spirit of *Fram* – 'Forward' – the name given to his Arctic ice-breaker. 'Splendid' was a common verdict, then, for the man of the moment but it is unlikely that an institution based on methodical consensus could be headed by such a dynamo who is essentially a short-term executive.

Inevitably, the emergency expedients of the Nansen era were followed by a period of administrative consolidation. Legal precedents were to be established with, in 1933, the League of Nations Convention Relating to the International Status of Refugees, and in 1938 a Convention Concerning the Status of Refugees. Only eight states ratified the code of 1938. The United States was never party to it, nor a member of the League. As for the prospect of refugees as something more than a transitory feature of a nervous world, the sabre rattle of Hitler's Germany had most states uneasy about the future.

The UNHCR: form and function

The new UNHCR moved into the 1950s stretching its limbs, confident that its place and function would be recognised as all-important. Its centrality in European affairs had given it headquarters in Geneva. The High Commissioner, usually from a patently neutral country and elected for a term of three years, was to report annually to the UN General Assembly through the Economic and Social Council. The founding statute of the organisation called upon governments to co-operate with the High Commissioner's functions in respect of refugee protection, and these were basically threefold:

* Immediate, though temporary, assistance and relief to those who were seen to need it.
* A search for permanent solutions to the refugee problem by assisting governments and private organisations to facilitate voluntary repatriation or assimilation in new national communities.
* All operational work to be entirely non-political, humanitarian and social in character.

Undoubtedly reflecting the expected transience of the refugee problem, in 1951 it was ordained that the 'competence' of the High Commissioner should extend only to those who experienced a 'well-founded fear' of being persecuted as a result of events occurring before 1 January 1951. It was certainly implied in the framing of work schedules that those events would be mainly European. This short-range, limited remit, understandable to most people at the time, was not refashioned ad infinitum until the follow-up Protocol of 1967 which, as we have pointed out earlier, was a measure to extend the work of UNHCR in time and geographically.

The 1951 Convention of UNHCR

The Convention was drafted inside three weeks, as we have said, though its full implementation took three years until April 1954, rather pointing up the realisation that refugees would be around for a long time to come. Twenty-six governments to begin with, and then double that number, were ready to go beyond the rudimentary legal protection and aid of the League of Nations days. Influenced by the Universal Declaration of Human Rights of 1948, there was ready acknowledgement of universal and basic human rights for any refugee. What was commonly expected to be a short-term engagement for the refugee organisation. is certainly visible in two aspects of the Convention. Deciding that only events before 1 January 1951 would count as arbiters for refugee status had much to do with the thought in the drafting committee that governments would not accept a blank cheque whereby they undertook obligations towards future refugees whose origin and numbers were unknown. There was a further uncertainty. From time to time, and certainly after the maelstrom of a world war, there is mass movement of people crossing borders and seeking safety. Would not these persons be outside the ambit of international law as it applied to refugees, since they would be thought not to be victims of an individualised fear of persecution? Otherwise, widening the classification inclusively would present another blank cheque, so it was thought. The matter of refugees fleeing war and civil disturbance has been discussed elsewhere than in Geneva. Member states of the Organisation of African Unity (as was mentioned in Chapter 1) adopted a wider definition in 1968 to include such victims. In the next few years, six of the forty-eight African states signing the convention were producing major population outflows. The 1949 Geneva Conventions relating to warfare do in fact provide for assistance to displaced civilian non-combatants, naming the International Committee of the Red Cross as supervisor and provider. The whole matter of non-combatant vulnerability and protection has grown hugely in the developing world since the days of framing the Convention, and must be one of the major concerns of all the aid agencies and of the United Nations. Furthermore, there is the nagging problem of how to cope satisfactorily with those civilians who are displaced within their own country, as was so tragically seen in former Yugoslavia. These internally displaced persons are not covered by the 1951 rule book since they have crossed no frontier. The Refugee Council in 2003 estimated that these unfortunates might number up to 20–25 million people in forty countries. They are searching for food and shelter from the violence that could be held as a 'persecuting', mind-numbing constant in a woeful situation. Whose responsibility is it to help them?

Inevitably, an organisation created fifty years ago and its red thread of a Covenant will be subjected to spotlights, mainly critical ones. With the flooding of people in the contemporary world, one question is regularly put. Why is the Convention, seen as the bedrock of UNHCR policy, not more concerned about mass movement? After all, when it was drafted, Europe was a place where queues of the displaced snaked across borders and stood pleading at most frontiers. A response to this, mainly from headquarters, is that the Convention set out to establish the rights of the individual, for in the end it was the individual as sufferer and complainant who had to be received, interviewed, assessed, and helped as one-in-need. Accordingly, it has to be so that the individual in mass migration is qualitatively different from the individual as persecution victim. Different approaches are needed, different tools used beyond the basic provision of some form of life-support machine. The Convention cannot be held responsible, as a brief, for failing to deal with situations it was never designed to address. This seems a reasonable point of view but it may not convince many, say, who work as immigration officers and who daily wrestle with the puzzle of distinguishing whose case is valid and whose is opportunistic.

Perhaps too much can be made of the previous shortcomings and other things which might be held to be missing from a document, surely drawn up when the contemporary world was dramatically different. In earlier days, as has been pointed out, we were less mindful of the problem of internal displacement. Nor did the Covenant mention at all the fact of gender-related violence so graphically obvious in today's world.

Purpose, policy and possibilities of reform

Over the years there have been numerous statements of purpose from the headquarters in Geneva. One of the most interesting pronouncements is that of 1988, by way of a general overview of form and function. An introductory note reminds us that for the organisation the 'persons of concern' range widely over women, children, the elderly, the stateless, 'returnees' and a greatly growing number of Internally Displaced Persons (IDPs). All these vulnerable, bereft people come under Geneva's 'globality of concern', a memorable phrase. And then a mission statement is reiterated in this way:

> International protection is a dynamic and action-oriented function, carried out in co-operation with states and other partners . . . to promote and facilitate admission, reception, and treatment of refugees and to ensure durable, protection-oriented solutions, bearing in mind the particular needs of vulnerable groups . . . [and the promotion of] conditions conducive to the preferred solution of voluntary repatriation.

As a statement of intent this makes interesting reading. The vocabulary is a contemporary one, putting into thoroughly positive terms the crucial need of action-to-yield-results in the shape of a partnership operation. Protection is to be durable, lasting, and that begs the question of direction of effort, nature of sustained work, and assurance of guarantee. There is a query, too, in the tail of the wording. Promoting beneficial conditions and the 'capacity' for improvement spearheads action but is voluntary repatriation a 'preferred' solution? It is worth considering this and the other proposed orientations for a moment.

Repatriation, voluntary or forced, is a tactic that has been much discussed. The easing of bipolar tensions around 1990 with the vanishing of the Cold War meant for UNHCR strategies the liberating factor of a 'fundamental change of circumstances in the country of origin'. It would now be no longer impossible or inadvisable for refugees to return to former communist countries. Repatriation appeared to be the only practicable remedy for loss of home and the burdening of the West, save for the proviso that UNHCR itself would carry out the assessment of safety for return. For many in Geneva and elsewhere, repatriation is a worrisome concept. Taking Them In looks like being superseded by Sending Them Home, without too many guarantees. Granted that eking out life in a tented camp is a short-term measure, though long-term it seems for thousands of Arabs evicted from Israel, the essential requirement for despatch from security must be a prompt and decisive assurance of steady and proper improvement and not a scramble for existence in a recently disordered land. Safety apart, what are the chances of 'returnees' reacquiring the dignity and the physical sustenance that are their right?

Then there is 'action-oriented', a commendable purpose, but it soon gets you into situations where there is a trade-off between conflicting values. There is a move forward from what has been termed 'value shaping', largely a didactic role, through pronouncements in covenants, declarations and protocols and the setting out of norms, and specific obligations. We can all see in the contemporary world that specific modes of action on the part of an international agency may not be realisable either on the grounds of uncertain security or on account of political manoeuvring, even of obstruction. There will always be the penalty area of the activists being branded as doing too much or not nearly enough. What happened in Bosnia or Rwanda or Sudan provides examples of aborted relief action. Basic relief operations in Afghanistan had to reckon with fierce opposition from local warlords. Operations in Sudan had to be suspended as the brutal conflict between government and rebels targeted even refugees and aid workers. Generally, the more active the fieldwork of UNHCR, the greater the prospect of political counter-activity and the difficulty of staying neutral. For many observers, action must be quantifiable.

Success and failure to achieve appear to have more to do with reckonable numbers, dates, times and priorities rather than with the less easily assessable preservation of human rights.

Again, protection-oriented is the position that successful refugee aiding will unhesitatingly adopt. A recent study of problems of protection (Steiner *et al.* 2003) is not at all sure that at present the UN organisation keeps protection boldly at the head of every agenda. Perhaps too often, UNHCR steps outside its own mandate to protect refugees, the 'core concern', to embark on additional developmental work and emergency aid when other agencies also out in the field could do things more effectively. Inadequate performance in Bosnia, where 'safe havens' for Muslims were overrun by Serb forces, was perhaps a result of being expected to do too much beyond the essential 1951 Convention brief. Does UNHCR have either the appropriate resources or the hard expertise? Is Geneva holding its own nostrum of 'catalyst in development' rather too closely to its breast? The 'fading prospect' for protection (Steiner *et al.* 2003) must be rigorously reaffirmed and reclassified if human rights values are to have absolute priority.

In a larger sense, any statement of mission from a United Nations agency such as UNHCR must take account of its inherent status. It has become very clear over the years that UNHCR has no political weight or authority in itself, rather, there is considerable moral authority and legitimacy. Geneva stands proud in a world where political considerations of priority and expediency often cut across humanitarian principles. No doubt it was not so much altruistic motives that led states to establish an advocate for refugees but rather the practical need to promote international and regional stability and as an aid to resolving movements of people seen as threatening peace and security and creating tension. UNHCR has often walked on a tightrope, 'maintaining a perilous balance', in the words of one commentator, 'between the protection of refugees and the sovereign prerogatives and interests of states' (Steiner *et al.* 2003: 4). The balance of legitimacy was carefully maintained in the first years after the agency's foundation through reminding states of their obligations, suggesting measures to cope with major problems, and by monitoring the implementation of internationally harnessed programmes and projects.

With the great increase in refugee flow in recent decades and a reactive unhelpfulness on the part of many states, there is a case for believing that the authority and legitimacy of UNHCR has been significantly eroded. Moral leverage is less effective. Whatever the present extent of decline, it was certainly obvious during the 1950s era of the Cold War when UNHCR fieldworkers had to stand and watch a major displacement of people moving from East to West, from the Bad Bloc of Communist states to the Goodness of the Free World. It served the geopolitical interests of the United States to prefer its own 'escapee program' to that of the more state-independent UNHCR. By dint of remarkable resilience and forethought in Geneva, UNHCR was able to enlarge the scope of its activities and build renewed financial solvency. Respect for its authority was recovered particularly in two ways; first, as mediator in toe-to-toe confrontation in the mid-1950s between the rival blocs where refugees from Hungary and Czechoslovakia were to be cared for; and second, through expanding its role and activities into the developing world of Africa and Asia.

The Convention, UNHCR and the prospects of change

It's out of date. No longer relevant to the contemporary world. These are some of the more general faults found in the Convention of 1951 by those who go on to instance the flood of millions today, the diversity of the hordes, the daunting problem of distinguishing bona fide refugees, the ease and relative cheapness of travel, and, perhaps cutting across the last point, the growth of a trafficking industry. There is a need for tighter control explicitly codified, it is said. In Britain, Prime Minister Tony Blair has spoken in 2004 of the 'timeless values' that UNHCR represents and which must stand; yet, he said, it was now time 'to stand back and consider its relevance in the modern world'.

Much of the debate has to do with the provision of 'temporary protection' which is regarded by many as a compromise way of dealing with the latest crisis. A score of questions can be asked. What means of protection can be contrived from the outside? Must there not be some form of custodial supervision externally imposed? Does protection depend upon an individual being able to return to former land and homestead and nothing less than that? Do not most 'returnees' need to be part of a returning family? How long is the protection supposed to last? A conflict resolved is but a stage towards eventual reconciliation, which may be slow to happen. Muslims back in Serb territory, Afghans returned to the former haunts of the Taliban are, by all accounts, not at all sure that unextinguished prejudice will permit them to stay. Temporary measures may help speedy egress from a life-threatening situation and perhaps effective reception and classification, but they surely lack universal and binding security. A project of this nature could even be ended at the direction of a state. Doors are easily closed if a lasting status is considered inexpedient. A point hinging on the notion of temporary is a changing interpretation of 'persecution'.

Is targeted violence against a population not persecution? In the present decade there has been violent, orchestrated harrying of Muslims in Bosnia, Albanians in Kosovo, Tutsis in Rwanda and the long travail of Palestinian Arabs. The 'agents of persecution', to use an old term, are no longer states but sub-states, rebels, militia. In the case of Rwanda and former Yugoslavia, one ethnic segment was pitched against another former neighbour. Around the world, the 'internally displaced' number, it is thought, is 20 to 25 million people in perhaps forty countries. Not having crossed any frontier, they were not covered by the 1951 Convention and are, in theory, still under the legal protection of their home government. Clearly, this is an anomaly which needs urgent redress. A feature of much of this displacement is the high proportion of women and children, again something not remarked upon by Geneva fifty years ago. Not until 1991 did UNHCR issue Guidelines on the Protection of Refugee Women, and in the last few years similar briefings have been published by Britain, the United States, Canada and Australia.

Reform of the Convention and the machinery to deal with the refugee problem is certainly an ongoing concern in the United Nations. At present, in Geneva and other centres, a series of 'global consultations' is being held with at least 140 states pooling the minds of diplomats, lawyers, NGO members, fieldworkers, and refugees themselves. However much tough pragmatism and antipathy dislodge ready humanitarian resolve, there seems, in this conference activity, evidence of a consensus to forge what one delegate described as 'new strategies for a restless world'.

Delegates discussing reform strategies, whether in New York or Geneva, will have ethical principles, 'good intentions', and political pressures from indigenous populations back home who are asked to share living space with 'incomers', who are victims of persecution or economic migrants. There are real problems here for governments to face where the electorate is ready to challenge legal and moral assumptions judged no longer relevant and where the media waits to get its teeth into ministerial indecision.

The Cambodia Project

No account of UNHCR's fifty years can be complete without a brief look at a major project on-stream during the last ten years, namely, that launched to resuscitate the country and people of Cambodia. It has been an undertaking expensive in costs and resources, detailed in every respect, a carefully coordinated approach, and one amply staffed, and in many ways it was to demonstrate the main lines of changing work with displaced peoples. Controversy about it has been plentiful, yet there is more agreement than dispute that what was attempted has taught valuable lessons to external interventionists.

First, a historical note. Cambodia was a French colony between 1863 and 1954, retaining a dynastic monarchy. The Second World War brought bitter feuding between rival power blocs but essential neutrality during the ensuing Vietnam conflict, although palace and people were courted by Moscow and Washington. A peasant insurrection in 1970 dethroned the ruler, Prince Norodom Sihanouk, and was then itself displaced five years later by an extreme, anarchic movement, the Khmer Rouge. Ironically named the Democratic Republic of Kampuchea, the brutal part-Maoist dictatorship of Pol Pot, 'Brother Number One', launched a fanatical, macabre and murderous cleansing of its own citizens, condemning them either to death in 'killing fields' or to primitive slavery. There was a wholesale panic-stricken trek out of the country by many Cambodians.

Second, a rescue was mounted by the nearby forces of Vietnam in 1978. Altogether, 8 million refugees, mostly squatters huddled in Thailand, were brought back to an asylum they recognised. The piece-by-piece restoration of safety in Cambodia took ten years to bring about. Presidents Mikhail Gorbachev and George Bush (Senior) sponsored Paris Accords in mid-1989 at which eighteen governments backed a form of trusteeship, mapped out strategies, and established the United Nations Transitional Authority in Cambodia (UNTAC). A peacekeeping force of some 22,000 from more than 100 nations was recruited. Sihanouk was reinstated.

Third, to set Cambodia back on its feet would be an extraordinary challenge. Almost half the population was living below the poverty line. One family in two included a widow and/or completely orphaned children. Something like 150,000 Cambodians were IDPs and there were no fewer than 360,000 refugees sheltering in Thailand. For all these, asylum seeking would involve a search for shelter, a job, food, assistance with healthcare and schooling. These goals must be realised in a climate of fear, make-or-break opportunism, and ubiquitous 'protection rackets'.

Fourth, the project would be multidimensional in aim and nature. Two main UNHCR objectives were explicit, namely voluntary repatriation and rehabilitation. Repatriation should, of course, be the consequence of real choice and careful decision with no hint that the refugee is being manipulated to return. As well as the closing down of some refugee camps and the chances of reliable transport there was every inducement to get home quickly after languishing twelve years in a Thai barbed wire compound. From the point of view of UNTAC, the bringing back of exiles would demonstrate popular support for proposed new Cambodian self-government and provide a reasonable and confident constituency for a general election. (Ultimately, the election held in May 1993 was a resounding success, with 90 per cent of those enfranchised turning out to vote.) It could be said that the refugee electors, tempting fate, were taking a political risk as well as one of human rights. Who could guarantee a political settlement essential to a stable future? Given the fragility of tolerance at high levels, how sure was it the feelings of reconciliation would trickle downwards?

Rehabilitation is the long haul of refugee settlement. UNHCR has long had the maxim on every agenda: 'No peace without development, no development without peace'. A former UN High Commissioner for Refugees, Sadako Ogata, had intoned the maxim in June 1995 as a multi-phased concept of peace, 'to include not only freedom from war but also from want'. Without that, she said, 'people may come home but for how long?'. The restorative process has to go beyond a promise; development will only succeed, again according to latter-day UNHCR belief, if development leads to popular 'empowerment', fundamentally based on partnership between those who provide the resources and those skilled enough to use them in planned fashion. Unfortunately, Cambodian partners were living from hand to mouth too often, with the thought that the Khmer Rouge might spring back at them like a wounded tiger. Cambodia had only ruined infrastructure pockmarked by 200,000 landmines. Few, if any, of the former rice farmers had more than 3 per cent of their lands restored to them. Despite an unpromising situation, a partnership was eventually created in the 1990s and is working slowly still. There have been sixty associates in a coalition made up of UNTAC staff, UN agency experts, a range of NGOs, and delegates from local towns and villages. Roads, wells, clinics, agricultural machinery and schools have been provided in the shape of Quick Impact Projects, each with three months to jump-start development. A first tranche of 9.5 million dollars enabled the Projects to begin, and they have got under way slowly. From outside, an observer sees refugees, in Cambodia and most other lands, unable to recruit trained and experienced 'partners' from their own ranks. If only one could be sure of more durable solutions to the case of the dispossessed – Lasting Impact Projects, in fact.

The Cambodian experience has taught the contemporary world a great deal and has, it could be argued, dressed idealism and optimism in more sober clothes. The generality of what we do for those who seek asylum is conditioned by a variety of often unpredictable circumstances on the ground. The next four chapters will serve as case studies of what can and cannot be done – for Palestinian, Balkan, Central African, Afghan and Iraqi refugees. In stark contrast, these studies show that going home is not always good news. Twenty years ago, Henry Kissinger published his thoughts about the many years he spent as a United States arch-mediator, jetting out of Washington to help resolve international disputes everywhere. Middle Eastern countries were frequently on his schedule. He had this to say about Palestinian refugees: '[they are] still treated as refugees in the UN, as terrorists in the US and Western Europe, as an opportunity by the Soviets, and as simultaneous inspiration and nuisance by the Arab world' (Kissinger 1982: 624–5). On another occasion, speaking to journalists after another weary bout with negotiators in Israel, he described what he had encountered in Israel as 'the world's biggest, deepest, and longest refugee problem'.

6   Case study 1
Palestinian refugees

The chapter will endeavour to trace the tortuous, sad story of fifty years of Palestinian exile. There will be a discussion in necessary detail of the roots of conflict and of the marginalising of around 5.5 million people (UNHCR estimate, 2001). Attempts by the UN and others to resolve what appears to be an intractable dispute will be outlined. The main feature of the story will be the way in which Palestinians have sought sanctuary in large refugee camps within Israel and in neighbouring Arab lands. Above all, there is a need here to be objective, for every dispute can only be understood and, hopefully, approached for resolution, if the concerns of all parties are carefully considered.

Roots of conflict

In the land of Palestine, now called Israel, Jew and Arab coexisted fairly peacefully for 4,000 years. This was certainly so during the centuries of being a province of the Roman Empire. Today's clash of interests and confrontation has much to do with outside intervention by Ottoman Turkey before 1918 and then by the United Kingdom, awarded a mandate by the League of Nations in 1923. British trusteeship was to last twenty-five years until 1948. A consequence of British involvement was the putting into effect of what was known as the Balfour Declaration, a set of promises by the British Prime Minister to Jews ousted from Europe by intolerance. A 'national home' would be granted those who went to Palestine and settled there among their Jewish kinsfolk. Somehow, the rightful claims for land and security on the part of the Arab residents of Palestine came to be overlooked. Legally and financially, and in every sense practically, the peaceful coexistence of two ethnic groups was put at risk. From time to time London sought resolution of increasing tension by trying out schemes for equable partition and immigration quotas which seemed to satisfy nobody.

The 1930s brought crisis to Palestine in the shape of shiploads of Jewish immigrants pushed out of their European homes by Nazi anti-Semitic purges and hatred. In one year – 1933 – 62,000 Jewish refugees arrived by sea and soon displaced Arab townsfolk and subsistence farmers. As war loomed in Europe, a conflict was gathering in Palestine as the new Jews ousted Arabs from the bright lights of the town and the best of their ancestral lands. It perhaps helps understanding of what was happening then and since to see a majority of people on both sides as, in a sense, refugees, the one displaced from Europe, the other evicted within his homeland. Jews, coming to the Promised Land as the 'Chosen People' (a promise made in the Bible and implied by Balfour) stood to defend themselves and in so doing stoutly asserted a right to return. (This is an issue to be returned to later in the chapter.) Largely in response to such a position, Arabs, termed 'non-Jewish' by Balfour, adopted a defensive posture and were no less fervent in insisting on a right to return. Thus, the scene was set for conflict between two rights, a conflict no external mediation has yet resolved. Confrontation over the same territory by those whose ownership must be incontestable makes for alienation. For decades now, those who know they are in the right have nowhere else to go. Everything is made worse by a majority in the two refugee sides, each fearing the threat of the other. Jews, particularly, feel menaced by encircling Arab states. Each has been made promises by would-be helpers in the outside world and when they act resentfully their attitudes and behaviour are condemned as fratricidal.

Palestine became Israel on 14 May 1948. The very next day, half-dormant tensions flamed into a succession of wars, each precipitating a flood of Arab refugees:

- May 1948 – five Arab armies invade from nearby states in alliance with Palestinian guerrillas (the fedayeen). After four weeks, the Arab host is defeated by a smaller 'hi-tech' Israeli force and Israel now acquires 20 per cent more land. Arabs are uprooted, 750,000 of them, and they trek to UN refugee camps.
- October–November 1956 – Israel, allied to France and the United Kingdom, confronts Egypt's President Nasser over Suez Canal nationalisation and sends an expeditionary force to Egypt. The battle is short and sharp and aborted at the insistence of America's President Eisenhower. UN peacekeepers supervise the wholesale flight of Arab villagers from the Sinai Peninsula to join their confrères in refugee camps.

- June 1967 – the Six Day War. Arab legions from Egypt, Jordan and Syria take on Israel. Once again, the Jews triumph, taking over more Arab land.
- October 1973 – the Yom Kippur War. Egypt and Syria launch a surprise attack, on a Jewish religious holiday. They are routed.

Armchair strategists and commentators among Jews commend the superior training and deployment of their own army, acknowledge the spirited tactics of the Arabs but conclude that the moral fibre of their own defence against all odds would always win the day.

International help for the Palestinians

For fifty years, the United Nations has been the voice of intended mediation moving predictably towards a position of censure. The early days held some promise when, shortly after the foundation of Israel, the UN set up a Palestine Conciliation Commission. Aptly named, the Commission members from the United States, France and Turkey came together in Jerusalem and later in Switzerland to coax enemies into an armistice and a further settlement. Progress petered out when Israel would talk only to separate Arab states and the latter stood firm on negotiating only as a bloc. Top of the agenda, as expected, was the position of Palestine's refugees now scrambling out of the war zone. The Commission was asked to 'facilitate the repatriation, resettlement and economic and social rehabilitation of the refugees and the payment of compensation'. Although the leading principle was the refugee's right to return to original homes, this was never acceptable to the Israelis. Nor would the Arabs yield on finally settling the refugee question as a precondition of even discussing other matters. A rather faint United States suggestion to Israel that perhaps 300,000 refugees might be allowed to return appeared to bring about Jewish contempt for the idea. A bolder attempt to push the negotiators into action was a firm declaration by the United States, France and, now, the United Kingdom that security and peace in the Middle East could only be made realistic if Israel's frontiers were held to be inviolable. This did not please the Arabs, who were aware that, in the border areas, Arab farmers were being systematically expelled from their own lands.

The Commission fell apart after four years. It has been suggested that the Arab world had never adjusted psychologically to the idea of a new state of Westernised settlers of alien culture becoming established in territory formerly occupied by Arabs. Prospects of lasting agreement were therefore dim. Neither side would envisage total agreement if the issue of refugees-in-the-middle were not settled.

One in four Security Council resolutions has to do with Palestinian refugees. The most urgent of them all was Resolution 242 of November 1967, which called on Israel to work for a lasting peace, to drop its belligerent claims on land and persons, to cease demanding and practising territorial acquisition, and firmly and effectively to settle the refugee problem. This Resolution is still not being implemented. One reason is that disputants interpret the wording in different ways. There is the basic incompatibility of stated rights and obligations. Put baldly, there is a world of distance between the Arab insistence that there will be no peace unless there is a grant of land and the equally stern Jewish rejoinder: 'no land without peace'. Again, for the Arab, repatriation to his sacred turf is a mission goal, however forcefully it is secured. For the Jew there can be no Arab going back without a state of peace. Moreover, complicating the picture is the stubborn refusal of Arabs either to emigrate in ordered fashion to other Arab states (not all of which would be keen to have them) or to return where both these movements would be on terms set by the Israeli government. To comply would make for the permanent triumph of 'gun Zionism' and signal a fatalistic acceptance of loss. Better to trumpet violent opposition through the stone-throwing confrontations of the *intifada* uprising and, most unhappily, through the none-too-rare havoc of suicide bombing.

A high point of international helping was the meeting of Israel and Egypt in September 1978 when President Jimmy Carter brought both rivals together at his presidential retreat of Camp David. There seemed steps being taken towards Palestinian autonomy and the possible eventual return of Arab refugees. Unfortunately, a promising start went into the ground, as did later negotiations in 1991 in Madrid, in 1992 in Oslo, in 1993 in Washington, and in Cairo in 1994. All of these trials at solution seem to run through three phases – the first of discursive 'sounding out', the second of 'reinforcement of positions', the third, and, usually, final one, is that of sitting back on the heels as the momentum (if not the goodwill) is short-lived and lost. Ideological holds and considerations of power advantage put brakes on progress. Indeed, both in 1978 and later, Arab historians and some Jewish ones have looked back at negotiations and thought that Israel's position included persuading the Palestinians to give up their right of return to original homes and properties inside Israel as the essential compromise for a peaceful solution. To go further, it has seemed to some commentators that the very problem of dealing with refugees has been pushed down most agendas. Any accord would sign away the rights of the exiles. Might the Jewish side in negotiations even look for a Palestinian leader who might be prepared to ditch return rights in exchange for a 'settlement'? Unhappily, too, and more evident in the past, there has been the seductive patronage of outside great powers, the United States backing Israel more obviously and, in Cold War days, the preference of the USSR for Arab interests.

Rights on both sides

A pre-eminent factor in all Israeli-Arab negotiations is the Right to Return, as we stated earlier. Amnesty International's website has usefully summarised the case of the Palestinians. The main position is that forcible exile is to be condemned. The right to return, based on international law, must always be acknowledged regardless of the circumstances in which people have been exiled, whether, for example, it was the result of a decision relating to an individual or the product of mass expulsions. Rather than a legal issue is the political fact that refugees became exiles sometimes in response to advice from their own Arab leaders: it was not always force majeure that expelled them. The extent to which they were being 'persecuted' is arguable; perhaps 'victimised' might be a more appropriate word. Even so, human rights were being violated where movement out of home was not entirely voluntary. An interesting further point is that covenants related to the Universal Declaration of Human Rights (1948) emphasise two interpretations of the phrase 'own country', a concept at the heart of repatriation of the refugee. In the first place, the scope of 'own country' is broader than the concept of 'country of his nationality'. In a formal sense, it is not limited to nationality but extends to any country with which a refugee claims to have indisputable 'special ties' and where he would not be considered an alien. The breadth in this distinction, nevertheless, might give rise to argument, say, in the case of an Arab, but it might offer a prospect of reception in more than one Arab state. Further to this meaning of linkage through 'special relationship', Geneva has ruled that the right to return applies not only to those directly expelled, and to their immediate families, but also to their descendants who have maintained what is termed 'close and enduring connections' with the area. Again, there could be argument but it might help the return prospects of Bedouin Arabs with their extended families. In regard to the specific case of Palestinian Arabs, Amnesty International in line with UN rulings believes that only a prompt and durable solution can repair the grievous harm done to the exiles. A lasting solution must address the security and environmental needs of both Israelis and Arabs, and rights are to coexist with mutual obligations. Last, and a point stressed by UN General Assembly Resolution 194 of December 1948, is that 'compensation should be paid for the property of those choosing not to return' and 'for loss of or damage to property' (for those who do elect to return).

Return rights are clearly contentious in their interpretation, the more so because they are uppermost in the refugee mind and seemingly less important in the debates of negotiators. It is also apparent that rights are invested with emotional feeling. Israeli offers to the dispossessed Arabs of an integration scheme where they could come back, on agreed conditions, into the mixed-group community have been spurned in the belief that Jews have not the slightest comprehension at all about something that is the essence of identity, the root of a legitimate struggle. Survival on those terms would be surrender, a humiliating way of living, much as the Bantustan which the Afrikaners offered the black people in apartheid South Africa. Why should Arabs, they ask, encouraged by the exhortations of such as Yasser Arafat and the Palestine Liberation Organisation (PLO), accept an 'humanitarian' enterprise, a sedative, rather than repatriation on full political terms favouring the precepts of their own national struggle? As for the insistence on Arab repatriation, there is an argument which ought to be approached objectively. What would happen if the 5 million Jews were to have over 3 million returning refugees foisted upon them? Even if the returnees came back by quota and in stages, would not the political and economic and cultural nature of Israel be irremediably altered and not peacefully at that? Not just Jews declare that return rights need to be weighed against the right to live in a cohesive community (where the extreme view is that that particular right must be defended, even violently).

Caring for Palestinian refugees

Years of talking have not done much for 3 million Palestinians evicted from Israel and languishing in downtown urban slums or scrubland refugee camps. Two out of three of them are jobless and half of them exist mainly on welfare handouts. A great deal has been achieved by the UN's Specialised Agencies working in the field and by the coordinated willingness of an array of voluntary groups, the NGOs.

Since 1949, a United Nations Relief and Works Agency for Palestinian Refugees (UNRWA) has cared for refugee victims of conflict. The amount of assistance given has been costly and hugely extensive, with some 2 million recipients scattered in camps in Israel, Lebanon,

Jordan and Syria. Two of these countries, Syria and Lebanon, between them have given asylum to more than 800,000 Palestinians. Originally, the approach was a first-aid engagement providing food, shelter, clothing and medicines, an active mission depending mainly on voluntary contributions from close on seventy governments and subsidies from the World Bank. Tented camps sheltered 750,000 displaced Arabs. As the target of encouraged self-sufficiency became realised, UNRWA shifted towards long-term developmental programmes and eventually was employing well over 17,000 Palestinians, almost half of them clinical workers and teachers. This has been a beneficial move but inevitably it has incurred criticism of political directions and influences made more difficult to counter by UNRWA's lack of a protection mandate. Israel's right-wing press has been suspicious of what are termed 'peace implementation programmes'. Will not Arab-favouring peace hazard Jewish security interests? Do not repatriation schemes lead to infiltration by former refugees, weakening the cohesiveness, again, of Jewish settlement? Undoubtedly, more of a protection mandate for UNRWA would worry, if not alarm, the more chauvinistic Jews, yet, on the other hand, there are Arabs who brand the organisation as too timid and too unimaginative in speaking up for the evicted. Why, they ask, do UNRWA and the UN's Security Council not condemn outright the building in the West Bank since 2003 by Israel of a miles-long steel and concrete separation barrier which effectively blocks off refugee access to schools and hospitals? They also wonder why international pressure could not have some impact on Israel's Prime Minister Ariel Sharon in the autumn of 2004 when he announced a dismantling of twenty-one satellite Jewish settlements in the Gaza strip, still with the separation barrier, while he bought time against extending refugee settlement in the West Bank on fairer terms. Such a strategy is thought expedient by Israel but it is inhumane. Critics abroad have not dealt easily with the role of UNRWA. If there is a 'gap' in protection because of the absent mandate, would not 'temporary protection' help, they suggest, to reassert the primacy of human rights for the exiles? It might do something to reassure certain Arab states that they would not always be burdened with a heaving flood of fellow Arabs seeking shelter and a share in a more prosperous way of life.

Palestinian refugees and the refugee camps

More than 3 million Palestinian refugees live in fifty-nine refugee camps maintained by the UN. The largest number of these unfortunates is in Jordan, and then they are in Syria, Lebanon, Israel's Gaza Strip and the Jordan West Bank, Saudi Arabia, Iraq, Egypt and Libya.

The camps in Lebanon are known to Arabs as 'the camps of shame' and 'the camps of despair'. In Jewish eyes, these camps are hotbeds of militancy. Today there are about 400,000 Palestinians there, the majority of them in UNRWA camps (see the Amnesty International website again). From the outside, they have a barrack-like appearance, ringed by barbed wire and guarded by Lebanese soldiers in watch-towers. Narrow, squalid lanes intersect huddles of ramshackle shelters built out of corrugated iron sheets. There is no dependable shelter during fierce summer heat or the blistering cold winds of a Lebanese winter. Twelve hundred people somehow exist in the Jal al-Bahr camp without an assured water supply, or a clinic, or a school. There is no sewage system. Regular shopping is not possible, only a rush to see what itinerant hawkers may be able to offer.

Lebanon has often declared that permanent settlement for all the refugees is not feasible, instead their stay is only a temporary one. In desultory fashion, they say that their refugees ought to exercise their legitimate right to return. Again, in unhelpful terms, refugees who are educated and professionally qualified are not permitted by law to prac-tise. Seventy-three occupational grades are ruled out for them. Whatever their schooling, they will do no better than manage as garbage men, cleaners and road workers. There is some demand for blacksmiths and house painters. Nor will the Palestinian be allowed to own any property, supposing he can accrue some assets and navigate legal jungles. There is no possibility of foreign travel and, if there were, then re-admittance would be debarred. Lebanon is a small country often racked by civil strife and with a small population suffering considerable political and ethnic tension. Their giving asylum to well over 300,000 Palestinians began with basic generosity shot through with the thought that there might be no discernible end to the burden they were taking on. Discrimination was born of that realisation.

Nearer the original Palestinian homeland are the Balata, Jenin and Jabalya camps in Israel's Gaza strip. Jabalya Camp sprawls over 1.4 square kilometres of arid semi-desert. Its latest head count seems unbelievable – 101,605. The biggest houses are each 40 square metres, put together out of wood, sun-dried brick and thin metal sheeting. They are packed close in smelly alleyways barely more than a metre wide. Seven out of ten of the men are unable to find work and they find it virtually impossible on $2 or $3 a day to sustain a dependable stan-dard of living for families crowded into two or three small rooms. What they do, according to Israel's government in Tel Aviv, is plot ruinous attacks on Jewish settlements and towns. They are the lethal swarm in the hornet's nest of Palestinian violence that Israeli commandos and gun ships will have to 'take out'. Tanks and heli-copters are deployed to destroy 'terror bases' but, of course, in their forays, kill and injure many harmless residents of the camp. Balata Camp is much smaller, with only 19,000 crammed into its hovels. Undoubtedly, there is every reason to expect the young men and many young women of such as Balata to don face masks and, equipped with M-16 rifles and Molotov Cocktails, dodge the 24-hour curfew to roam the streets of Jewish settlements, soft targets for their rage and despair.

Another Lebanese camp is that of Jenin. This camp has been the subject of an intensive study by two researchers who published it in April 2002 (Glacaman and Johnson 2002). The statistical profile they present makes for disturbing reading. Jenin housed 9,104 refugees, according to a 1997 census, but UNRWA believes it may be of the order of 13,000. In an area of 1 square kilometre, 1,614 households compete for survival. The most vulnerable, women, children, the infirm and the elderly make up six out of ten residents, while four out of ten are under the age of sixteen. More than 95 per cent of the Jenin people are registered refugees. A great many of them have swarmed in from hamlets nearby which can be seen from the camp, petrified by the Israeli 'snatch squads' and continual gunfire. It is safer in the filth of the camp lanes, although many in-camp refugees mingle with out-of-camp relatives for family occasions and feast days.

When there is peace in Jenin Camp, there is progress. Generally, economic conditions are in line with the developmental programme goals of UNRWA. Some 70 per cent of adult males there work out of the camp in vineyards and on orange farms, in chain stores or laundries. Twenty per cent of young people are students. However, the frequent round-the-clock curfews and the occasional punitive raid by the Israeli Army restrict movement and work routines and drastically erode weekly incomes.

Women cannot avoid malnutrition, miscarriages and anaemia. The chronically ill do not find medicines easily available or affordable. There is much determination in Jenin, of a resentful kind, but it is strength of body that is more important than strength of resolve. Visitors to Jenin from the outside world are astonished that so many near-destitute thousands are so easily overlooked by a world which could do far more to sustain them. Visitors also come away quite often with a surprise that there is ambition and forward thinking alive in the rubble and decay. Is it not a sign of resilience and of exercising that other right, the right to live, that seven out of ten parents, when interviewed, are keen to see their children go on as students? Peace would make a tremendous difference, a generation at a time, to the suffering of Palestinian exiles.

The right to play and the right to dream

A last word is that of refugee children from the Lebanese camp of Chatila (Shatila), near to the capital, Beirut. This camp was attacked by Israel in 1982 in a hunt for violent activists and there was great loss of life among the families. During 2000–1, Betsy Cook, a history teacher from the American Community School in Beirut, was completing an oral history project that had included on-site work in Palestinian refugee camps locally. Seventeen Palestinian refugee children had been invited some time earlier to write about themselves. A number of the interviews had already been published (Cook 1999). Personal anecdotes such as these make for moving reading and are an apt conclusion to an account of Palestinian refugee life. Muhammed Daud, aged fourteen, has this to say:

> When I work in Chatila, I don't feel miserable or curse my life, because all the children work here and child labour isn't something strange . . . Then I started to ask myself why I wasn't playing and running in the fields the way those other children were . . . Why am I living this tiring and miserable life? Why do I have to work to live? I know why: because I come from the camp, because I'm a Palestinian refugee. That's why I'm asking to be granted my civic right, and I hope this timeless message will be seen by everyone around the world. I want to play, not work.

Then, the whole group chimes in unison:

> I dream of a family that could care for me and give me affection and a house outside the camp with a green yard in a place without alleyways.
> And I dream of finishing my schooling if I should want to and of choosing what I want to be, even if it's a garbage collector.
> But I'm afraid that my dreams will hit up against the walls of the camp . . . I'm afraid when I dream that my dreams will hit up against my reality, my being a Palestinian refugee with no rights. And I ask myself, am I really denied the right to dream? And I ask the world, don't I have the right to dream?

These children could surely say, as does the Palestinian poet Mourid Barghouti (Barghouti 2004: 62), returning to the West Bank after thirty years in exile: 'The long occupation has succeeded in changing us from children of Palestine to children of the idea of Palestine'.

7   Case study 2
Balkan refugees

Ask most people what their first association is with the word 'Balkans' and their reply will allude to internecine hostility, fratricide and, almost certainly, the suffering of refugees on an immense scale. They may, of course, remember the beauty of the tourist trail and the warm welcomes they and others encountered. Media reports they recall are different in association – the blood-spattered market-place raked by snipers, the village burned out by house-to-house combat, the horrors as mass graves revealed what has become known as 'ethnic cleansing'. Firm in the memory, also, is the intemperate rhetoric of Balkan politicians and army chiefs and the sad witness of the press correspondent.

The case study in this chapter will focus on part of the Balkans, namely Yugoslavia, known now as the Former Republic of Yugoslavia and by the acronym FRY. Again, we all remember the magnified barbarism of ethnic contest, the primeval slash-and-destroy of genocidal incidents, the swelling floods of displaced people. Much was seen and talked about in regard to international intervention to prevent, shield and rescue. The UN, NATO and a great array of NGOs arrived, attempted to help where logistics proved virtually insurmountable, and they departed often in disarray. Now, in 2005, there is a ceasefire, a return of many thousands of refugees, and a putting into place of a set of complex political and humanitarian arrangements. The Balkans, as most of us expected, was to prove rather impossible to manage, certainly, from the outside. What remains questionable is the extent and direction of reconciliation. To come to any understanding of the refugee situation in FRY it will be necessary to look at the past, the present and the likely future in some detail.

The making of Yugoslavia

Yugoslavia, in some respects, is an artificial creation. At the Congress of Berlin in 1878, the great powers in Europe redrew the map of the

Balkans to serve their own imperial interests while conceding some limited autonomy to two new countries, Serbia and Montenegro. At Versailles in 1919, the master powers redesigned the remnants of the Austro-Hungarian and Ottoman empires, mainly to benefit their own political and economic concerns and to a lesser extent the nationalist sentiments of such as Serbia, Bosnia and Croatia, all elements of the new Yugoslavia. This new creation, a federated Kingdom of Serbs, Croats and Slovenes, was to bring together in uneasy cohabitation Serbs, Croats, Slovenes, Macedonians and a range of émigré Slovaks, Greeks, Magyars, Albanians, Italians, Turks, French and Germans. Hyper-idealism as the Great War ended was to produce there and elsewhere in Europe a crop of weak new states fashioned out of ethnic groups whose traditions were mixed and whose mutual affability and readiness to work together were not calculable. Ironically, today's political scientists refer to this process as 'Balkanisation'. Certainly, in Yugoslavia unity was likely to be wafer-thin in a landscape making physical intercommunication difficult, where there were three official languages and two scripts, and where there were three religious followings, 29 per cent Roman Catholic, 36 per cent Orthodox Christian, and 14 per cent Muslim.

Popular discontent within a slow-melding community was always predictable during the 1920s and 1930s, as one ethnic group would try to lord it over the others. The advent of the Second World War predictably was to dismember the frail unity of Yugoslavia. A brief attempt at neutrality between 1939 and 1941 was shattered by invasion from Nazi Germany and the picking over of the spoils as Germany, Italy, Hungary and Bulgaria seized prime agricultural land. The Yugoslavian king and government were exiled to London and ruled only tenuously over a land fragmented and ruined. Fortunately, something was saved as 100,000 disbanded Yugoslav soldiers took to hills and forest with their weapons, as partisans.

It was a partisan commander from Croatia, Marshal Josip Broz Tito (1892–1980) who eventually was to bring Yugoslavia back from the grave, though not yet in any unified fashion. From 1942 to 1945 he conducted war on two fronts, against the German army of occupation and, poignantly for him, against fellow Croatians whose puppet regime allied itself with Hitler. Tito's strength of purpose was probably the only thing that enabled Yugoslavia to survive the war and then, after liberation in 1945, to try to weld together the discordant elements in the population. It has been reckoned that, during 1941–5, one tenth of Yugoslavia's population were killed, many of them by fellow Yugoslavs. It was certainly Tito's resolve and obduracy that kept his Marxist state separate from the Soviet Union, indeed, not linked to either side during the Cold War. With his death in 1980 and the collapse of communism throughout Europe, nationalistic factions began to assert themselves as Belgrade's central government devolved into six independent republics, each with its own Deputy President steering a separatist and nationalistic course. The republics were Serbia, Slovenia, Croatia, Bosnia-Herzegovina, Macedonia and Montenegro, with the autonomous provinces of Kosovo and Voyvodina. 'No longer one Yugoslavia – it's six of them, now', claimed the radical press in the capital, Belgrade. There was legislation to protect minority rights. Tito played off different ethnic groups in an attempt to create a stable balance of power. Even so, Yugoslavia's disintegration was gathering momentum. After three and a half decades of communism and authoritarian rule, ideological and economic differences were contributing to tension. In one federal election, the year after the death of the unifying Tito, there were 100 opposition parties campaigning for ascendancy, usually with an ethnic bias.

The shattering of Yugoslavia

Combustible elements burst into flames in June 1991. Serbia, headed by the nationalistic Slobodan Milosevic and proud of retaining communism, became ever more chauvinistic and possessive about 2.5 million Serbs living in other republics who needed to be 'rescued'. This would be done, not by bringing them home, but by expanding as a Greater Serbia to envelop them wherever they were. Areas such as Croatia and Bosnia must be 'cleaned' of their non-Serb people. This was the beginning of what was to become a huge refugee evacuation of threatened territory. Motorised columns bit deep into the northernmost republic of Slovenia and then Croatia. Jet aircraft swept the skies and bombed villages. These were two republics which had cocked a snook at imperious Belgrade. Five months later, Bosnia-Herzegovina was hit by Serbian invasion and pillage. Thousands of terrified country people sought shelter in the backwoods or trailed out of the war zone into neighbouring asylum. The more enterprising and affluent were able, by ship or plane or car, to reach Italy, Austria and Germany.

European politicians, on the whole, were divided in their response to the flaming of Yugoslavia. Germany, certainly, endorsed the proclaimed independence of Croatia and Slovenia and readily offered sanctuary to those who fled in the winter of 1991. The United Kingdom and France leaned towards thinking it rather premature to stress partition since this perhaps was not in the best interests of an increasingly divided nation such as Yugoslavia. Nevertheless, as the toll of political victimisation began to mount, there was every prospect that a tremendous refugee crisis would grip Europe and force governments to do something. The tactics of this Balkan war seemed not centred on the defeat of military opponents so much as the terrorising and expulsion of civilians. In 1999, in face of the massive refugee crisis in Kosovo, NATO launched a military strike to create conditions that would allow for a safe return by thousands of refugees. Was not forcible expulsion on ethnic lines the last word in civilised breakdown? Was it conceivable that any multicultural nation could ever descend to such depravity? What might the appalled world be able to do about it? It seemed as though the zealots of Serbia were the prime instigators of discriminating violence and forced removal, but there were indications that old jealousies and scores were about to be drastically settled in many regions of the country. A vengeful sorting out on these lines even appeared to be occurring in Bosnia, home of ancient harmonious traditions, where 43 per cent were Muslims, 32 per cent were Serbs, and 18 per cent were Croats. Their President Isetbegovic was Europe's sole Muslim head of state. Nemesis arrived in the spring of 1992 in the shape of a well prepared Serbian blitzkrieg. Towns went down like skittles. Bosnians swarmed for any refuge they could find. The Muslim majority made up the bulk of the casualties and the refugees.

Mediation by the outside world

Three initiatives were shared by the UN and by a number of governments. First, there were attempts at a distance to build a peacemaking structure by diplomatic means; second, to intervene on the ground with a peacekeeping force; and third, in the field and again by means of intervention to rescue and protect refugees. Diplomatically, by the summer of 1991, the first international peace proposal was in draft with a proposal to stabilise disparate Yugoslav tendencies by consolidating a federation of the six republics. Serbia refused to risk its dominance. Altogether, there were to be eight main peace plans between September 1991 and November 1995, with Lord Carrington and Lord Owen (David Owen) from Britain and Cyrus Vance from the United States as the chief initiators. Schemes for partition into a collection of republics found little favour with disputing Yugoslavs. Nor among them was there ready agreement to have both the UN and NATO arrange a ceasefire, supervise disarmament, patrol 'safe' corridors through devastated territory, and escort relief convoys and refugee crowds. Proposals for 'territorial adjustment' to refashion borders more in accord with ethnic distribution and, hopefully, as a means of staunching refugee flow, generally hit the ground. The leaders of rival elements required cast iron assurances as to the security of the people in their charge. Bosnians wanted to be a sovereign state and not a UN protectorate. The Serbs knew that time and the winter were on their side, despite an arms embargo imposed upon them by the European Community (now the European Union). They appeared contemptuous of a deal where their putting an end to fighting would be rewarded with the lifting of UN sanctions against Belgrade and the pumping in of several million dollars to revive the economy. Controversy in a wider Europe wondered whether any settlement with maps and figures would do much to punish Serbian aggression and in any way reward those who had stood their ground against it. What rationale and reassurance could be given to those scheduled to move elsewhere? And who then would have the necessary authority and even-handedness to explain and carry out partition? Would rearranging the Balkans yet again bring peace and amity? There was little sign that Balkan leaders, proud and unilateralist by preference, would ever take kindly to the proposed schemes of outsiders.

If diplomatic moves proved unavailing, peacekeeping operations had to be mounted. In succession, a number of arrangements were put into effect. Intervention to hold the ground between contestants and to protect the innocent living and moving between them held two main requirements in balance, the principled and the militarily pragmatic. There should be no compromise in the moral duty to offer asylum and save lives. But how was this ideal to be enforced? By common consent among soldiers and experts, any enforcement must be a short-term measure. Moreover, the protective role of such a force must stop short of making it in any way a party to conflict. Most certainly, if the force were not a major undertaking politically and tactically it would be more of a protective *presence* than a protective *power*. The drawing-boards and conference rooms of those who felt obliged to intervene breathed life into a number of deployments. The names given to these schemes point to their stated main goal:

- 1992 – formation of United Nations Protection Force (UNPROFOR) and its despatch with the help of NATO on relief convoy duty. Strength to grow to 75,000. This is a peacekeeping role independent of UNHCR, trying to cope with the aiding of three million FRY refugees.

- 1993 – mandate of UNPROFOR expanded to surveillance of six 'safe areas', and the 'open city' of Sarajevo, the Bosnian capital, as well as the monitoring of refugee movements. The force would be scaled down to 40,000 eventually.
- 1994 – an improvement with a four-month truce between Serbia and Bosnia. Part of UNPROFOR was to be restyled as the United Nations Confidence Restoration Operation (UNCRO) working in Croatia. With anxieties about conflict in Macedonia as refugees pour out of it, a new force is recruited as the United Nations Preventive Deployment Force (UNPREDEF).
- 1995 – in November, the Dayton Agreement is signed by the presidents of Serbia, Bosnia and Croatia, while they are holed up in a United States Air Force base in Dayton, Ohio, and put through an intensive process of 'tough peace contracting'. There should be a discernible reduction in refugee flows. Also this year a new force is to be formed with a fresh remit – the Implementation Force (I-FOR), charged with overall implementation of the Agreement. NATO will command its impressive resources of 60,000 seasoned troops.
- 1996 – in December, a Stabilisation Force (S-FOR) succeeds I-FOR. Half the size, it will take further the next peace-building phase of stabilisation and the focus of redirecting refugee movements out of harm's way and into areas where supervised resettlement can be tried. Rules of engagement are, as far as practicable, meant to be neutral and 'robust'.
- 1998 – Serb forces attack Kosovo in the south of Yugoslavia and this ranges an Albanian majority against both resident Serbs and the invading army. There is much savage violation of human rights by Serbs and even by Albanian ultra-nationalists. Some 350,000 people are ruthlessly displaced.
- 1999 – NATO launches an air campaign over two months against the Serb aggressors. This does not restrain a further invasion of Kosovo and a terrible harrying of Muslims. Virtual depopulation sends 400,000 refugees trailing to Albania, 240,000 to Macedonia, 69,000 to Montenegro. An improvised NATO airlift brings 90,000 out of Kosovo for eventual temporary asylum in twenty-nine countries. NATO and Russian forces enter Kosovo after Yugoslavia accepts a peace plan requiring all forces to withdraw. Refugees flood back despite the peace plan.
- 2001 – Macedonia, in conflict for six months, now accepts a peace agreement brokered by NATO and a number of European states.

The protection of refugees

In all of the above, and in retrospect, one can acknowledge the rationale and the faith in ordered, negotiated progress. Outside of Yugoslavia there was a mixture of deep human concern over the fate of so many innocent victims, just as there was a good measure of criticism, even of incredulity, as to the ambitious mandates given slender international forces. The questions were many. Essentially, imported moral power was confronting dug-in firepower, facing it down, perhaps, and certainly trying to find an end to inhumanity, in a situation where civilians were being pounded to dust and despair. Who was to do what, and where, and when and how as the crowds panicked and the graves were dug? The stages in conflict resolution – protection, confidence restoration, implementation of agreement, stabilisation – must have looked commendable in theory as they were etched several thousands of miles away. The stages and the objectives brought up particularly against one rock-hard issue, that of time. Would the protective-direction of all these deployments be anything other than temporary protection? (This issue of temporary protection has been raised in an earlier chapter.) In such a fractured and unstable situation as FRY presents, how credible can it ever be that temporary protection offers any guarantee of dependable and lasting asylum? Can such a continuum be imposed by external pressure and its agents? Apart from the time factor, a pressing problem for all governments in Europe was to do with space. Was it best to attempt staunching refugee outflow by bringing relief supplies to the besieged inside Bosnia, for example, rather than incur the hideous problems of extracting them for despatch to unfamiliar places? Most UNHCR fieldworkers were inclined to favour a first aid approach, either in a familiar home locality or, where that was not possible, in a neighbouring host country. In fact, both the first aid approach and the extraction operation were hazardous, with relief workers in flak jackets dodging artillery, small arms fire and minefields. All the warring parties were liable to regard UNHCR as a legitimate military target that prolonged the battle and fed and bandaged the enemy. There was a problem with trafficking, where refugees, uncertain about when and how to leave, would be 'put in contact' with ex-army officers, Muslim middlemen and Croatian or Macedonian gangsters prepared to 'arrange' easier (but expensive) travel.

Although much international press blamed Serbs for their barbarism, all the contending parties were guilty of atrocities. Almost 2 million refugees fled the Balkan turmoil, the greatest displacement of population since the Second World War. Two out of three were less than twenty years old. Many thousands were killed or wounded. Anti-personnel mines claimed many lives. Hostages were forced to mask the movements of infantry, and weaponry was sited close to hospitals, schools and churches. Food and water supplies were often systematically targeted and destroyed. Relief convoys were frequently impeded and shot at though they were clearly marked. Incidents of this nature led to public appeals for stronger military support in which effective humanitarian action was possible. On the other hand, the Red Cross and the Red Crescent (working in Muslim areas) tried to preserve their neutrality consistently by refusing to accept armed escorts. Some air surveillance was tried, along with the rather uncertain alternative of food drops. Operation Provide Promise flew many missions from Rhein-Main in Germany and Ancona in Italy in a coordinated enterprise using American, French and German aircraft. Slow-moving transport planes were often in jeopardy since they were vulnerable to ground fire and effective delivery was difficult and dangerous from low altitudes. UNPROFOR was faced with a catastrophic scenario of at least 2 million refugees and the resuscitation of those who had been maimed, raped or bereaved. It was almost impossible to deal with an emergency such as the sixteen-month siege of Bosnia's capital, Sarajevo, where 10,000 civilians were killed, over 58,000 wounded and where 60 per cent of industry was crippled.

European governments, faced with a flood of refugees, were divided in their response. Germany offered asylum to 425,000 from FRY, Switzerland 85,000, Sweden 70,000, and France 25,000. Other states allocated quotas to parcel out the homeless and insisted on visas and residence permits. The United Kingdom's first reaction was tentative and rather unhelpful in urging asylum seekers to find harbour in a nearby 'country of first asylum' such as Austria, Hungary or Czechoslovakia. Visa restrictions were in place to begin with there, nor were families readily acceptable. Later, refugees were granted asylum but the procedures were slow moving. It was not until 1996 that significant numbers of asylum applicants from FRY began to be granted refugee status. It was growing clear that there would be no early end to conflict and displacement. Italy, once so involved in the Balkans, appeared to regard refugees as unwelcome immigrants once numbers began to swell. They did have a problem of intercepting and containing many hundreds of young people chancing an Adriatic crossing in leaky boats.

The UN in 1992 had mandated UNPROFOR to protect a number of so-called 'safe areas' in Bosnia. These were only lightly safeguarded, compared with the 'safe havens' for Kurds in northern Iraq protected by allied firepower on the ground and by the wings of the US Air Force scrambled from airfields in Turkey. The policy was undone by Serbs who had little compunction in firing on famished people in the 'open' towns of Srebenica, Mostar and Gorazde. Serb refusal to lift the sieges brought a NATO air strike of doubtful effectiveness. This appeared to be turning into a no-win situation. If the UN were to evacuate these helpless people, would it not be carrying further the ethnic cleansing of Serb fanatics? Yet, by penning refugees in glorified prison camps, the UN was reinforcing notions of ethnic difference which would lead to summary eviction.

Refugee repatriation

Repatriation of refugees from FRY was an objective much discussed as battle areas were being depopulated. To take one example, Bosnia, with a tradition of tolerance, was keen to have back 1.2 million displaced Bosnians. While many of them were sheltering not far away, in Croatia, in requisitioned accommodation and perhaps hoping for a passage home, the Muslims among them were anxious about Croatian prejudice. There was now a plan for a Croat-Muslim federation but many families were still most reluctant to return to villages from which they were evicted. (Ten years have elapsed since the Dayton peace accord provided for refugee return to places of origin and for safe-guards that resettlement there would be practicable.) Mainly since 1998 there has been a concerted drive in Western Europe to effect large-scale repatriation of the displaced. To begin with, there were mammoth relocation problems. Germany, for instance, was to return 250,000 Bosnians (half of them children and Muslims) and it was found that their destination would be in Serb-occupied areas. Many arrived in their former villages to find property requisitioned and hatred among former neighbours. How would they survive? The German repatriation effort was in danger of breaking international conventions which do not permit the refoulement of refugees. Quite clearly, now that the Balkans is no longer in the midst of civil conflict, the problem of rein-tegration in a sorely wounded society is immense and one for the Yugoslavs themselves to sort out.

Many of those encouraged to return to FRY had been severely traumatised by their experiences and made anxious still further by the uncertain status offered them and their families under 'temporary protection'. Arrived in Britain, they found it difficult to adjust to life there and almost impossible to find any sort of employment. It was often impossible for them readily to face going back to a half-destroyed country where they might soon be made unwelcome. An improved situation came with the new Labour government in 1997 reassessing temporary protection and confirming status as refugees for the majority of the Yugoslav asylum seekers. This revised policy was in line with a realisation that not only was conflict unlikely to end in the short term but that the outcome for both those who had stayed or left was distinctly unpredictable. Whitehall clearly had in mind, according to commentators, the issue of predictability, for the European Union had ruled in May 2001 that:

> Persons receiving temporary protection must be able to return in safety and dignity in stable context and in conditions where their life or freedom would not be threatened on account of their race, religion, nationality, membership of a particular social group or political opinions and where they would not be subjected to torture or to inhuman or degrading treatment or punishment.
>
> (Feller *et al.* 2003: 12)

There is also the special situation noted in the UNHCR Handbook where a person may have been subjected to very severe persecution in the past, in which case there can be no grounds for 'cessation of status', namely, ceasing to have refugee status, even if fundamental changes have occurred in the country of origin. Women and children, severely abused and traumatised, and who would face further discrimination, cannot reasonably be expected to return. These are individuals who deserve being picked out of a larger group whose return prospects may be very much easier (Feller *et al.* 2003: 76).

Reintegration and peacebuilding

Yugoslavia's population fell by half during the war years 1991–5 and nearly half of those people were displaced. By the end of the fighting, most of the countryside was segregated on ethnic lines. Something like two thirds of housing was uninhabitable. Schools and hospitals had been put out of action from time to time. There would be millions of dollars needed for rebuilding. In the flush of a pacification agreement, the Dayton accord of 1995 had secured the parties' agreement to respect the rights of refugees and IDPs and to facilitate their return. The lead role by way of liaison was naturally given to UNHCR. Also in the field were 250 or so voluntary groups, NGOs in the main. Visitors to the resettlement areas were sometimes critical of the infighting that seemed to go on when the groups were lobbying governments for funds and competing with each other for access to local administrators. In such a war-torn location, no resettlement programming can ever have been easy. Two things raised difficulty after about 1999. First, a number of NGOs indulged in unilateral initiatives without coherent planning or coordination of policy and action with UNHCR and the UN system. In the early days, when an NGO was unable to get through to an emergency where people were being trapped, starved or shot, it was only the NATO soldier, rifle in hand, who could respond meaningfully with food and tents. NATO, however, was a party to the war, with a dual role, military and humanitarian, and was seen, certainly by Serb and Croat brigades, as an interfering agent and morale-raiser. Second, though it was not always so, refugees tended to be treated as passive objects of pity rather than as dignified, capable participants in a shared reconstruction enterprise. Oxfam was one of the organisations able to encourage and train refugees as co-workers in specific rebuilding projects.

Refugees returning frequently encountered bureaucratic red tape which gave them scant recognition despite the formal assurances of the Dayton procedures. Coming back to the farm often meant, first, the eviction of squatters, then the repair of buildings, the clearance of what land was still cultivable, and above all the confirmation of ownership and settlement of volatile disputes. Those rural communes which put their heart into resettlement were financially rewarded. Perhaps the most difficult problem was to accelerate house building programmes. There were schemes for temporary rehousing such as the Collective Centres, dormitories in converted factories and office blocks, which had to accommodate nearly 6,000 Bosnians in 2000–1. Makeshift hutted camps were not very comfortable during the long months of a Balkan winter, nor were they entirely safe from marauders seeking revenge.

The road home

The pace of returning Kosovans was dramatic in scale. In the spring of 1999, about 850,000 had fled their homes. Within weeks of negotiated peace, 90 per cent of them who had sought sanctuary abroad were moving back, although UNHCR could not guarantee their safety. The majority had returned voluntarily though 9,000 had been forcibly returned from Western Europe. These 'returnees' were part of a mass movement, spontaneous in many ways, representing thousands of individual decisions by people determined to take the road home whatever the risk. There were those in authority in Kosovo and among UNHCR who were uneasy about a mass movement as something which would be too soon and too difficult to cope with. After a decade of poor industrial investment and creaking public utilities, and with 65 per cent of people jobless, Kosovo was hardly able to look after its residents, let alone an inrush of half-starved newcomers.

Return after 2000 was now being facilitated by the new Republic Srbska government in Belgrade. There was a pledge to resolve the refugee crisis, relaxing legal obstacles to regained citizenship and permanent residence. In 2001 this humane gesture received a reward of a 1.3 billion dollar aid package from the European Union. Bosnia, the same year, followed this example, officially welcoming no less than 730,000 Bosnians home and also receiving a dole of 5 billion dollars. War criminals, generals and political leaders, including Slobodan Milosevic, were extradited to the International War Criminal Tribunal in the Hague in June 2001. Not all those returning were able to face up to the implications of their decision. A number of long-term refugees simply lacked the willpower to make up their minds. They hesitated over applying for resumed citizenship, so it seems, since that would entail leaving the safety and warmth of the 600-odd Collective Centres and having to fend for themselves in an unkind environment.

There was a larger meaning to the issue of whether or not to return. If re-establishing links with what was once home is in prospect, then it must offer security and a reasonable lifestyle. Yugoslavia, even before the 1991 crisis, was in a state of economic transition from central planning to a market economy on more democratic lines. Living standards were improving measurably, with trade, transport, private enterprise and energy resources all conferring significant benefits on communities and individuals. Thus the outbreak of hostilities in 1991 was quite disastrous. In addition to civilian casualties and the wholesale uprooting and evacuation of communities, there was severe damage to property and looting. Billions of dollars would be needed to kickstart industry, and for the resuscitation of basic amenities. With the onset of a rebuilding phase likely to last a decade or so, after the peace of 1995 there began a period of 'donor fatigue', as a number of states backing reconstruction made cuts in their overseas spending. Neighbouring countries in southeastern Europe felt constrained to trim their budgets because of the collapse of their Yugoslav trading outlet. Inevitably there was a ripple effect, with the majority of those returning facing a hard and uncertain future.

The Balkan refugees: what next?

There is no definite conclusion to this case study of fifteen years of conflict and eviction. Optimistic observers talk of the multitude of the brave going home to take up the traces once more. They find reassurance and hope in the stories of ethnic groups (once 'all Yugoslavs') slowly and delicately learning to live next door to one another, farming adjacent fields, treading the same streets, shopping in the same market. The pessimists cite the difficulties of travel, reception, and a calm resumption of what was useful and peaceful and good. Most agree that in the light of the demonic nature and scale of what happened in a Balkan heartland it may take years before wounds heal. A recent word from UNHCR touches upon the essential of man-to-man reconciliation as part of reintegration:

> The Balkan region is a bewildering mosaic of hope and despair . . . While hundreds of thousands of civilians are rebuilding their lives, equally large numbers are staring into the abyss . . . Grandiose global strategies may ultimately depend on thousands of tiny individual gestures.
>
> (UNHCR, *Refugees*, 2001, vol. 3, no. 124)

For the returning refugee, must not mutual respect and tolerance be elemental in the chemistry that brings neighbours together? Somehow, somewhere, sometime the Yugoslav must follow the advice of Robert Burns – 'Then gently scan your brother man'.

8   Case study 3
Rwandan refugees

This case study has something in common with the preceding two, namely an account of vast human distress and refugee movement as the inheritance of conflict and then, as large numbers return, the persistence of tension, latent and unresolved, in an unsettled homeland. The refugee, coming home, has not too much to live for, either as a Palestinian or as a former Yugoslav. It is now the turn of Africa to provide examples of slaughter and eviction on an incomparable scale. Demonic upheavals in that continent are estimated to have torn 25 million people from their homes and forced them to trudge across desert scrubland and steaming rainforest looking for any sort of shelter. Most countries in contemporary Africa have witnessed horror – Angola, Burundi, Eritrea, Ethiopia, Liberia, Côte d'Ivoire, Rwanda, Somalia, Sudan, Western Sahara, Zaire (now the Democratic Republic of Congo). No longer is the refugee only someone in a distant photograph. Africans are attempting to gatecrash Europe, totally desperate, and in their tens of thousands. This case study focuses on just one of the great refugee centres, Rwanda, where conflict and spillover erupted ten years ago and where the country is now settling down into tenuous normality.

An account of Rwanda's devastation makes unhappy reading. In 1994, and within thirteen weeks, an estimated 500–800 thousand Rwandans perished, victims of civil war and genocide. Two million fled the country and almost one million wandered aimlessly, unable to escape. Africa has been crippled by internal warring but nothing is comparable to the suffering of Rwanda. This, particularly, must have been in the mind of Britain's Prime Minister, Tony Blair, when he declared two years ago that 'The state of Africa is a scar on the conscience of the world, but if the world focussed on it, we could heal it'. Africa remains on a knife-edge and Rwanda has been on the periphery of hell.

Rwanda is one of the smaller states in Africa, not much smaller than its former colonial master, Belgium. Just south of the Equator, it lies within the macro-basin of the Great Lakes region, Lake Tanganyika, Lake Victoria and Lake Edward. Land-locked, it is a country of mountains and high plateaux. Nine out of ten of its 7 million people are subsistence peasant farmers, cultivating tea, coffee and fruit on fertile soils, with two to three crop seasons annually. A census in 1991 listed a majority of Hutu people at 91.4 per cent, a minority of Tutsi people at 8.2 per cent and a small remnant of Twa hunter-gatherers at 0.4 per cent. Almost half the population is under the age of fifteen with a life expectation of fifty-three years. Sadly, 20 per cent are infected with the HIV virus and AIDS.

Geography apart, it is in the historical context of Rwanda, perhaps, that clues may be found as to its recent turmoil. Two elements recur, authoritarian rule and oscillating relationships between the main ethnic groups, Hutus and Tutsis. Rwanda's scenic beauty and fertility and equable tropical climate have not blessed its people with much that is dependable and peaceful. Two imperial masters marched in to help themselves to a benevolent environment and they subjected Rwandans to exploited serfdom. Germany came in first between 1894 and 1914 and Belgium took over in 1915. It suited colonial governments to see their subjects ordered by a semi-feudal system of chieftainship where people were given land grants in return for obligatory military service to the tribe. Although the Hutus and the Tutsis intermarried and shared their fields, there was for many years a growth of tension between the two when colonial governors favoured the minority Tutsis. Rwanda was put under a League of Nations mandate in 1919 though nothing was done either by the League or the Belgians to provide for a settled community with fair shares for all. Indeed, it was the Belgians who compelled Rwandans to carry an identity card proclaiming their ethnic origin.

Fight and flight

The Second World War brought the end of colonialism in Africa, though Rwanda only slowly achieved independence in 1962. Hutu power was now in the ascendant, menacingly so in the eyes of many Tutsis who took themselves off as refugees to Burundi, Uganda and Zaire. In brief, the beginnings of Rwandan tension and division had already been evident, with the exiled Tutsis grouping under charismatic leaders as fervent freedom fighters aching to repossess their old lands. They formed a band known as the Rwandan Patriotic Front (RPF) and by the late 1970s were harrying the Hutu strongpoints in their homeland. There was now the making of a civil war between the

Hutu government in Kigali, Rwanda's capital, and the Tutsis intent on border warfare and enthusing their brethren inland. Equipped with weaponry from France, the RPF launched a full-scale invasion of Rwanda in 1990. Again, those who could escape the battle fled as refugees, several hundred thousand of them. At times, in the view of United Nations observers, the situation flared into 'mindless violence and carnage' with nobody outside able to stop it.

It was as late as 1993 before external mediation was able to achieve anything tangible about the Rwandan drift into communal collapse. That year, in Arusha, Tanzania, a contact group from the Organisation of African Union (OAU), Belgium, France and the United States managed to draw up a comprehensive peace accord. An end would be put to three years of fighting, and steps taken to bring about shared government in Rwanda. Unfortunately, radicals on both sides rejected any compromise. The RPF was insistent that the 1 million Tutsi refugees who had left since 1959 must be allowed to return before any agreement could hold. Hutus were not inclined to accept that at all.

As the situation darkened, the United Nations Security Council authorised the formation of a monitoring mission, the United Nations Assistance Mission for Rwanda (UNAMIR). In fact, the mission was hampered from the outset. Commanded by a Canadian, General Romeo Dallaire, the group was labouring under an inadequate six-month mandate which called for protective capability and all-round surveillance, yet it was denied manpower and appropriate equipment and supplies. Twenty nations had backed the mandate but failed to ensure its effective translation into action. Dallaire was forceful in lamenting 'the inexcusable apathy of governments' unable to see that the forceful expulsion of Tutsis was a violation of human rights and a powder keg that would surely ignite. There was no peace to patrol. There was no available force to secure peace. What was the point of UNAMIR 'supervising' the breakdown of peace? As refugees poured out of Rwanda, UNAMIR felt its hands were tied, something that the vicious oligarchs in Kigali could recognise. They had a plan for genocide, a plan that was already obvious to any visitor or close observer. The Red Cross could see a 'major humanitarian catastrophe in the making' in 1993. To be quartered in Kigali, according to one of its fieldworkers, was to be in a 'claustrophobic, airless hell'. Moreover, the hellishness that was obviously brewing was being fed, quite illegally, by arms dealers in France, apartheid South Africa, Israel, the United States and even Albania. They were supplying the Hutus with rifles, artillery, rocket launchers and mines. French military advisers were on hand in Kigali.

The killing operation went into top gear in April 1994. UNAMIR, reduced from 2,500 to fewer than 300 men, could only look on initially in disbelief. The peak of Hutu frenzy was reached on 6 April when an aircraft carrying the presidents of Rwanda and Burundi was brought down, it was said, by RPF missiles. The incident ignited what tinder was not already alight. Kigali's radio station broadcast the most virulent attacks on Tutsi 'snakes and cockroaches' who must be exterminated. Moving through the streets of the capital and out into the country went the death squads, young militiamen to be known now as the *interahamwe*, 'those who fight together'. They were to spearhead the killing programme with machete knives, small arms and clubs. Their victims were the recognisable Tutsis, men, women and children who could be slashed and burned. Captured, a Tutsi would be forced to reveal the whereabouts of relatives and friends. Any moderate Hutu, aghast at the mayhem, would also be despatched. Within one hundred days, the tally of killed reached a rate five times that of the Nazi death camps. According to one or two survivors, it was not so much the gunfire that the cowering Tutsis feared as the chanting and whistling of the group approaching, intent on mutilation, rape and murder.

How could they ever resort to such mayhem is a question much aired then and since. What peculiar motivation ever changes that neighbour of yours into a sadistic maniac? What is the meaning behind this confession of the Rwandan smallholder, interviewed by the BBC, that 'all of this came like madness – how did it get into my mind – you could not be normal – attacked by the devil'? Whatever the psychological elements in eventual inhuman behaviour, it was more the result of political 'management' rather than the outcome of tribal warfare.

'Nothing but people'

Over against the bestiality of the killing fields, Rwanda was the scene of complex swirls of human movement. As the blood ran, so Tutsis in the main, with some less extreme Hutus, all took off to Tanzania. There were an estimated 400,000 of them, swelling soon to a million or so. They were racked by semi-starvation and even dysentery and cholera. The sanctuary they found in camps thrown up by UNHCR and Oxfam was almost too crowded and too foetid to endure. Within two months of the genocide's beginning, cross movements of refugees made Rwanda an impossible place to control. The Hutu government had sought to evacuate a number of vulnerable Hutus from the fighting, the elderly, women and children, all to be escorted to Burundi and Tanzania. As they were leaving, something approaching 700,000

Tutsi refugees, including children born in exile, were returning to Rwanda, mostly from Uganda. These were the New Rwandans, promised a peaceful place in a scheme of things that displaced the old Hutu administration with a Tutsi one, assured by the firepower of the RPF, in control of Kigali. Towns, villages, refugee camps, one by one, were now falling into RPF hands.

One reflective observer of all this movement was Maureen Connolly, overseeing UNHCR field operations in Tanzania and visiting Rwanda late in April 1994. 'We looked up at the Rwandan hills', she said. 'There was nothing but people. The entire African landscape was awash with people all headed our way'. Through a nearby border control post, 'two hundred thousand refugees crossed into Tanzania in twenty-four hours, the fastest and longest exodus of refugees in modern times'. There was nothing but people and not much help from outside powers, leaving everything to the almost impossibly stretched resources of UNHCR and a dozen-strong clutch of NGOs. The World Health Organisation and the World Food Programme, United Nations agencies, had to make Herculean attempts to keep the mass of refugees alive. Established now in the Kigali seat of power, the new Tutsi government did not care to help Tutsi returnees, nor did they hide their suspicion of all outside help. It was true that neither they nor UNHCR were confident of distinguishing the victims from the killers when both were languishing in tented refugee camps. Were the camps hotbeds of guerrilla intention, safe havens for murderers? Were genuine refugees in peril from reprisal from neighbouring inmates? Kigali's move to cull potential troublemakers was, at one point, to close all the camps and let loose hapless refugees into bush country or back to the lawless streets of towns. More clumsily, in 1996 the RPF and its eager Congolese allies attacked a number of camps indiscriminately, looking for armed elements. Refugees witnessing the outrage paid with their lives. Whatever the circumstances of peril within and peril without, the camps saw one refugee dying each minute.

Camp security was ostensibly the responsibility of UNAMIR. Their straitened resources had to prevent intimidation and violence, to protect relief workers from frequent assault, to husband stores and convoy deliveries. An impossible task. They certainly would do their best to promote voluntary repatriation. There was a good response to this from Tutsis, but as recently as 2004 some sixty to eighty thousand Rwandans were still in camp, or scattered over the border in nearby states.

Hopefully, by the end of 2005, voluntary repatriation would have melted away the forlorn thousands waiting either in camp or over the

Rwandan border. Two unfortunate circumstances have been making prospects of easier movement more difficult. In the first place, major host states such as Tanzania and Kenya have tightened border entrance and departure and called for forced repatriation of their refugee crowds despite the insecurity and violence so evident in Rwanda. Second, and perhaps an understandable follow-on to the first decision, such host states have shown marked unwillingness to take in any more Rwandans. The refugee camps are regarded apprehensively by these governments as being launch pads for cross-border incursions and as training centres for guerrillas.

Alongside UNAMIR, the relief work of UNHCR proceeds at a record pace. There are twin objectives, first, to work for repatriation and, second, to care for those on site whose numbers are also eroded by disease and malnutrition. 200 million dollars has already been spent on rudimentary housing in the vicinity of camps scheduled for closure. There seems a dreadful irony in one agency worker's statement that there is now 'room to move'.

Those who returned

Hanging on to survival, the returnee was often trapped between the Hutu farmers who had helped to decimate his family and fellow Tutsis returned also from exile who had got back first to take possession of land and house. Even so, by 1997, 1.3 million Rwandans were thought to have made the journey home. Most of them had endured a twilight existence in hills or forest, staggering out years later into a country they barely recognised. 'Can it be safe to come home yet?' was the question on all lips. 'Is my neighbour one of the *interahamwe*?' There was much suffering, with a widow looking after six orphans and a grandfather scarcely able to reckon what remained of his skeletal family. In every family there were grim stories of those members never accounted for: they were among the 'disappeared'. There were success stories such as those, back from Canada or Britain, who were able to open a small business in Kigali, a place hardly recognisable from the trauma days, and one resplendent with new hotels, mobile phone shops and internet cafés.

Return and reconciliation

Reconciliation is interesting in theory. Going beyond resolution of a conflict, particularly that of a fratricidal nature (as in Cambodia, El Salvador, Afghanistan or Northern Ireland), reconciling a fractured community involves working for an integrated alternative. That will depend upon individual and group preparedness to make concessions for the sake of tolerance and civilised behaviour. How far is it possible to help advance this process of remediation? Is it realistic to expect that all aspects of a conflict are purged and eliminated in a community so drastically riven as Rwanda? For the thousands who have sought peace on their return, is it feasible to mount a programme of 'assisted reconciliation' on the lines, say, of what was being done in Cambodia and South Africa? There is perhaps a grain of truth in the assertion from Belfast that 'ten years of a conflict will take one hundred years to resolve it'. Reconciliation in its most complete sense may take rather longer. The issue of reconciliation will be discussed later in the retrospective Chapter 12.

Reconciliation cannot be expected to come about either quickly or easily in a community that has been catastrophically melted down. Several barriers to any progress with mutual movement and understanding are obvious. Kigali's weak government is tainted by its association with RPF guerrilla ideology and battle. The President, Paul Kagami, heads an administration that has become only slowly more credible after nine years of transition. The presidential reputation is not helped by his being suspected of involvement in the shooting down of the Hutu president in 1994, but more to the point is his reluctance to engage with the more peaceful elements in both tribal groups. 'There is too much of the gun belt in the presidential entourage' is one foreign diplomat's recent view. It was advice from South Africa, in the wake of the riddance of apartheid, that encouraged Rwanda belatedly to institutionalise a reconciliation process despite the forbidding climate of intolerance in the country. In 2000, Kigali established a National Commission for Unity and Reconciliation. The first step was to consolidate democracy by allowing eight different political parties rather than the confrontation of the two traditional rivals. Refugees would return to an 'enabling society' rather than a severely prescriptive one. It is too early to say whether an attempt at reconciliation-by-design will have any hold at all. Practicability will decide the likelihood of coexistence schemes taking root. What is unlikely to succeed is one theoretical proposal, imported by United States academics, to relocate Hutus and Tutsis in a pilot 'togetherness cluster' in a rather remote undeveloped country backwater. Refugees will not want to return to that shared future.

More positively, there are signs that the new Rwandan government is beginning to hold to account many of those who brought their country to its knees. Initially, in 1994, this was a clumsy process, with the RPF clapping 120,000 suspected killers in jail. There were refugees, both Hutus and Tutsis, among that number. By degrees, many of them were released after five or six years, an act of quasi-leniency which satisfied nobody. Eventually, though, and after discussion with UNHCR and the United Nations, it was proposed in 1996 to set up an International Criminal Tribunal for Rwanda. There would be a bench of internationally recruited judges who would sit for two years in Arusha, Tanzania. Their brief would be to examine and judge cases of reported genocide within Rwanda. The definition they would employ would encompass acts committed with intent to destroy, in whole or in part, national, ethnic, racial or religious groups. Acts would include conspiracy, public incitement and attempts to bring about genocide. Crimes committed as part of a widespread attack on the civilian population on the basis of national, political, ethnic or religious grounds would be taken into account. Most of the miscreants expected to appear before the Tribunal would represent the general population whose behaviour had so often been inexpressibly appalling. Richard Goldstone, Chief Prosecutor for the Tribunal, in his acceptance speech, spoke of the grinding vision of countless refugees and the barbarism they encountered. 'Ordinary people', he said, 'are capable of doing terrible things, given circumstances, given propaganda, given historical hatred, and given fear'. A tangible sign of earnestness in account-taking was the early appearance before the judges of four Rwandan former cabinet ministers. These senior Hutus, one of them a former prime minister, were charged with incitement to murder. They were accused of overseeing the distribution of imported weaponry. According to the prosecution, these four had gone about replacing local authorities that opposed the massacres with others reputedly more sympathetic to the killing schemes. All four, in the event, pleaded guilty to genocide and were sentenced to life imprisonment, an international punishment rather than the Rwandan death penalty.

In addition to the International Criminal Tribunal, Rwanda did have a traditional way of meting out justice. These were the *gacaca* courts. The word denotes the lawn on which village elders for years have gathered to settle tribal disputes. After extensive searches among the returning refugees, suspects were rounded up and taken to the scene of their original accused crime where they would be confronted by their victims. This, at least, was the homespun theory though, understandably, it was not taken too seriously by visiting lawyers. Where was the impartiality of such a court? Would witnesses be dependable for their objectivity? What sort of punishment might there be to fit the crime and who would exercise it? Most refugees, court or no court, feared discrimination, even revenge, among those they met on return, and the *gacaca* gathering might make their position identifiable and worse.

Mutual trust and a future

'Without mutual trust there can be no future.' These were words that the Rwandan Parliament heard from Kofi Annan, the visiting Secretary-General of the United Nations, in May 1998. Rwandans had to trust each other and the world outside had to trust Rwandans. It was a neglectful world for which there could be no excuse. He went on: 'Genocide is a paroxysm of horror from which there is only the longest and most difficult of escapes. The international community and the UN could not [in Rwanda's case] muster political will to confront it. The world must deeply repent its failure.'

Kofi Annan took pains to emphasise what he has termed the 'sea-change' from immediate relief to long-term development. In Rwanda, the gap is there between the two approaches, largely because of the enormous strain the care and resuscitation of refugees puts upon personnel and resources. Planning and operations have to shift from tactical first aid caring to strategic sustainable development over carefully calculated periods of time. It is vital above all that the direction and rate of development seen in usable buildings, first-class communications, sown crops, guaranteed harvesting, literacy campaigns – all the elements of orthodox development 'engineering' – satisfy the Rwandan's immediate expectations and persuade him to stay. Rwandans trust those who provide and the providers trust the consumers and those now able to stay at home. These points are among those aired by the Secretary-General as he toured a re-emerging society and economy.

Pragmatically, the lines of Rwanda's future have been sketched out by UNHCR in a document with the title 'UNHCR Country Operation Plan: Planning Year 2004'. The plan's main objectives are listed as follows:

- To promote voluntary repatriation of an estimated 80,000 Rwandan refugees.
- To provide training and funds to the new Rwandan National Council for Refugees (NCR) which will take over the determination of refugee status from UNHCR as soon as possible after 2004.
- To provide adequate shelter for refugees in liaison with nine UN Specialised Agencies and some fifty NGOs.

- To promote and organise resettlement schemes as 'durable solutions' for Rwandan and other refugees.
- To conduct nationwide re-registering of all refugees in Rwanda.
- To prepare for the return of Congolese refugees (at least 32,000) to their own country and to facilitate the repatriation of Rwandan refugees to areas deemed safe.
- To help prevent environmental degradation in refugee camps and transit areas.
- To assist government provision of protection and material assistance to all refugees hosted by Rwanda and to continue the search for durable solutions to the refugee problem.
- To take account, in relocating refugees, that urban and rural refugees have differing needs and preferences.

(This UNHCR planning was to be done in association with the World Bank and the International Monetary Fund.)

In regard to the forward movement of this planning, there are a number of noteworthy developments in the Rwandan scene. In May 2003 there was a general election with the government winning 95 per cent of votes cast. A new constitution for the country was then tabled and approved. In 2004 there was put into place a remodelled and coherent scheme to make sure that returnees did not have to compete unfairly for what was limited land space. There are signs that Hutus and Tutsis are fitting into this reasonably well. Also in 2003, and a heartening advance in amity, agreements were concluded between Rwanda and a number of host countries to work out quotas and dates for voluntary repatriation. The planning has been seen as 'very businesslike at last'. The repatriation routes and destinations would not be related to the old refugee camps, which would be dismantled after careful survey of their inmates and after a staged programme of disarming all former combatants.

Numbers still matter. During 2003, upwards of 3 million Rwandan refugees came home. As the planning proposals of UNHCR indicate, the return of others from other African territories would be given utmost priority and should have been mainly cleared by the end of 2005. Development, once again, is the crux of the fortunes that the returning refugee will have in mind. This time it is Rwandan enterprise and control that is overseeing the process, with the Rwandan National Council for Refugees steering a five-phase programme – disarmament, demobilisation, repatriation, resettlement, reintegration. The more successful the programme, and the firmer the security situation becomes, the sooner NCR will see the scaling down and phasing out of UNHCR.

In every possible sense, the end of Rwanda's internecine torment displacing millions is the beginning of a whole new revolution for the country. Towards the end of 2003 something occurred that heartened a multitude of the younger Rwandans. Their country's football team qualified for the Africa Cup of Nations. Sport perhaps is helping advance a fresh spirit of sharing and peacefulness. Today's searching of the internet using the keywords 'Africa sport' spotlights Rwandans training for soccer matches, and visits by international rugby players and Ugandan sprinters in November 2004. Alternatively, rather than take a seat in the stand, one may use a cheap flight from Heathrow to search for gorillas and chimpanzees. Such things point to a more settled Rwanda, if not an entirely reconciled one.

9 Case study 4
Afghanistan

This case study considers a country attacked, wasted by war, and virtually emptied of its people. For two decades the media have reported the turmoil there. Huge relief operations have been mounted. The world constantly talks of a dreadful past, an unsettled present and a future where foreboding must be mixed with hope. Afghanistan's trauma is four-phased, namely external attack; the follow-up of an authoritarian regime; a second redress, military and political; and a final settlement on paper but hardly in practice. This terrible scenario, if it does not teach us many lessons, certainly begs numerous questions which this chapter will raise by way of feeling the way to answers. Above all, how is it that the millions who left desolation have so definitely returned to what were lands of chaos? In their time of trial and removal, had we treated them as humanely as they deserved? Could we more effectively have helped them to take the road back? Is it possible to do more for repatriation and resettlement in war-blasted lands? Where eviction and flight are the result of open conflict it will be necessary, once again, to look at the whole story to understand its consequences.

Afghanistan: roof of the world

Never a stranger to conflict, Afghanistan has been victim of contest between neighbours such as Russia, China and India, and, since the third century, investment by Arabs, Persians, Mongols and Turks. During the last two centuries, Tsarist Russia and Imperial Britain played a 'Great Game' where at stake was ultimate control of a buffer land. Certainly, Britain strained every nerve and calculated every feint and move by way of controlling the routes down into India and its suzerainty there. At times this meant an alliance with dynastic chiefs or the despatch of a punitive expeditionary force. Things were settled uneasily in 1907 with an Anglo-Russian entente and later in the 1920s when Britain felt better seeing an Eton-educated King Amanullah reign in the capital, Kabul. His cautious attempts to educate a notoriously unruly people, to play off the diverse interests of patriarchs and fundamentalist clerics, and to modernise an equally wild environment were approved of in London, when nearer the scene it was never easy to manage tribal feuding. At least, a potential trouble spot, perched invitingly at the gateway to Southeast Asia, was kept out of the Second World War.

It was a radical republican element, schooled in anti-imperialist sentiments, that deposed the monarch in 1973. Their rather bookish socialism sought a new deal for their countrymen. Poor, illiterate and oppressed, Afghans are still 99 per cent Sunni Muslim but they share little else. A land which is mainly mountainous, with peaks reaching 25,000 feet (more than 8,000 metres) is forbidding to till. Infertility, though, is balanced by suitability for growing poppies, the source of opium and its derivative, heroin. This is the major source of a mega-rich product where, predictably, a few drug overlords, unsoiled by hard labour, have pocketed the proceeds, which constitute 60 per cent of the country's GDP. Transition to Nirvana was never going to be easy or equably managed for the ordinary Afghan working his heart out on the land with no prospect of acquiring industrial skills.

The roof blows off Afghanistan

Things came to a head in 1978 when Afghan socialists, once again learning their craft abroad, seized power in Kabul and set up a pseudo-Marxist administration. It was going to be difficult to steer the ship on such an unproved course and the shipwrecked institutors of a new Afghanistan were forced after only twelve months to appeal for help to their patrons in Soviet Moscow. Fifty thousand Red Army troops with tanks and aircraft came over the border in 1979 and installed a puppet regime in the capital. There was the risk that Soviet intervention might be seen as ideological aggression, a calculated thrust in global strategy for reducing an 'imperialist military bridgehead' rather than a rescue of a fellow-communist state. The campaign went badly for Soviet Russia. Afghan guerrillas, the *mujahadeen* ('God's soldiers') exchanged their village homes for dugouts and gunsites and soon got the measure of the Soviet forces. Armed by Pakistan, the United States, China and Egypt, this was to be another 'Great Game' in the Cold War. One in five Afghans became displaced by gunshot and likely starvation. The country's schools, hospitals, factories, roads and farms were destroyed.

The year 1985 brought a breakthrough in a dogged struggle. Then, the liberal, imaginative leader of the USSR, Mikhail Gorbachev, began to negotiate a ceasefire and a settlement with the aid of the United Nations. There were signs that the USSR sought to be rid of a situation that had all the makings of a Soviet Vietnam. The permafreeze of the Cold War was slowly giving way to cautious collaboration between the former adversaries of East and West. Not until 1988 was mediation successful. After nine years of conflict, the Geneva Accords emphasised two objectives, military disengagement and reconstruction of the country. Moscow acknowledged it had been 'wrong' to trespass and so endanger the security of the whole Southeast Asia region. There must now be international guarantees to safeguard Afghanistan's independence as a neutral, demilitarised state. Above all, the plight of 6 million Afghan refugees, sheltering mainly in Pakistan and Iran, must have immediate resolution. Priority was to be given to this rescue operation in the hands of a new administration in Kabul backed by international agreement and force. Unhappily, the new administrative framework was weak from the start, fracturing hopes of unified progress and reconciliation.

Taliban and the vacuum of power

If Nature abhors a vacuum, so did Afghanistan. Edging into overall power in Kabul around 1992 was a group of mullahs heading a rescuing mission whose function was to rid Islam of poisonous Western influences. They were the Taliban, a mix of pious clerical intolerance and strength from battle-hardened veteran soldiers. Under their strict code of utopian fanaticism, the Ministry for the Propagation of Virtue and the Prevention of Vice, with its own squad of police, would secure public obedience and deal ruthlessly with dissension and uncomfortable behaviour among 'subversives'. There would be no doubts or debate allowed, no music or gambling, no cinema or TV, and for women total inequality and subservience. Within the master's ranks there were those who cultivated reliance on Kalashnikov automatic rifles and terror tactics and were allying themselves by 1998 with a cadre of willing terrorists, the al-Qaida front. Resources of arms and money here were considerable, directed by a millionaire civil engineer from Saudi Arabia, Osama bin Laden. The direction of Taliban thought and action was to bring them into conflict with the United States and its allies.

Political shifts in Afghanistan which were altering drastically the prospect of a unified and secure state did not altogether deter the return of refugees. Of the 6 million or so who had lived through the Soviet attack and occupation and the disorder that ensued, and then fled abroad, some 2.5 million had returned by 1992, leaving an estimated 1 million in Pakistan and 1.5 million in Iran. The returnees almost took their lives into their own hands, coming back to a place where narrow religious convictions underpinned government and assumed precedence over people's well-being. In particular, several aspects of a changed Afghanistan must have struck them and, frankly, put them in peril. One in three Afghans had had life completely disrupted and been displaced. Those who braved it and took up the old traces were to come upon the shell of their abandoned home village and pastures lethally strewn with landmines. Hardly any of them, in any case, had survived two decades of conflict without physical injury and a shattered family. The countryman who was used to fending for himself with the aid of the clan could generally pick over a bare existence, even though one of the worse droughts of the century had ravaged the countryside. Those who took up life again in Kabul and other towns had to manage without drinkable water, habitable accommodation and dependable food. In every sense, the Taliban had restored law and order at the expense of human rights. Evident, too, for those who attempted to resume family life was the gross male-female discrimination of the new era. The returnee now encountered a sexist split where girls and women would not be permitted to work or to attend educational activities. They must be shrouded in a *burka*, a head-to-toe black garment with a narrow eye-slit. Extended families now often had a woman at their head. In Kabul it was reckoned that 30,000 widows, short of status and resources, were now trying to cope with large families. In so many respects it must have been disorientating for those who had experienced generosity, understanding and wider horizons in the countries of asylum.

Displacement is a keyword to describe the nature and scale of the refugee problem in Afghanistan, just as it is in the Balkans, in Rwanda and among the Palestinians. While it is rarely straightforward to distinguish the persecuted refugee from the economic-main-chance migrant and those who seek sanctuary from natural disasters, there is general agreement that most of those who flee these places do so because they are forced to when violence and discrimination are directed against them. Where the toll of those displaced runs into millions, the catastrophe is made all the more distressing if the multinational community as well as the country-in-despair are slow to implement substantial relief measures. Behind the headlines of the world press, there has often been reluctance in commitment and implementation, revealed as a lethargic 'donor fatigue'. In Afghanistan itself, the ironically styled Ministry of Martyrs and Refugees did very little to match up to the urgency of a collapsing populace. On every hand, fighting and lawlessness disrupted relief work, yet these operations could have had far more telling rationale and collaboration. There was every reason for the UN's *Chronicle* publication in May 2001 to put the challenge in terms that might have been even stronger: 'The sheer magnitude of the population in need, coupled with limited resources and logistical constraints have significantly limited collective ability to reach all those in need before they have no option but to leave.'

The year of years: 2001

Most outside observers have seen this year as a progression from bad to worse, with just a little light glimmering in the distance. The Taliban decided in July 2001 to ban poppy cultivation. Internationally, this met with approval since a poppy derivative, opium, is used both as a medicine (in laudanum) and more widely as an illicit narcotic. Unfortunately, the edict only led to more displacement of people, as the landless collectors of the poppy harvest now lost their only income and had no choice but to take refuge in overcrowded camps or make the long trek to Pakistan. They were not so much refugees as deprived victims of a hasty government policy. From outside, the US State Department coupled economic and humanitarian ideas and decided to allocate $43 million to help the unemployed poppy farmers. (There were, of course, American protests about this from anti-narcotic groups.)

The Taliban were losing ground, quite literally, by the middle of 2001. Their kicking in anguish against the 'interference' of Western aid agencies meant destitution and death for those unable to leave. For the Taliban itself the crunch came with the blasting of New York's twin towers on '9/11' in 2001 and the impassioned US linking of terrorist outrage with al-Qaida, Osama bin Laden and Afghanistan. Phase two of Afghanistan's febrile history now began with another external attack, this time from an outraged United States.

As refugees streamed out of a Kabul targeted by the US Air Force, the enormity of this came home to Pakistan and Iran. How would they ever be able to cope with up to 6 million evacuees? In earlier years their 'open door' policy towards refugees had been consistent with Islamic traditions of proffered asylum. Borders now must be shut in Iran and Pakistan, as the frontier zones grew black with people, in August and September. The Pakistan government, so generous hitherto, now put the issue of refusal quite plainly. With a worsening economy, huge extra immigration costs were not to be borne. The 'donor fatigue', so evident elsewhere, would place an unsupportable burden on Karachi. An additional mass of entrants would entail grievous upset in the country's employment, accommodation and public order sectors. As for refugee status, how would it now be possible to screen the victim from the opportunist heading for the bazaar? With such a crisis in the offing, UNHCR called on Pakistan and Iran as neighbours to admit, protect and help the forlorn knocking on their closed doors. Government ministers in Pakistan's Ministry for Foreign Affairs were regretful but plain speaking. 'If donors have donor fatigue', they said, 'then we have asylum fatigue. If donors' patience with the Afghanistan situation has run out, then so has ours.' They added that they were not as cold-blooded as they appeared to be, but 'it's just that we have reached our limit'. They would, of course, have to be careful to avoid the charge of facilitating refoulement. From a different perspective, homeless Afghans were quoted as reacting to ministerial coldness by declaring that they would rather return than stay in a place where they would 'lose their dignity'.

There could be little dignity in the reception arrangements already in hand for Afghan immigrants in Pakistan. The camps put up to house them were overcrowded to an incredible extent in July 2001. Killo Faizo had 3,000 inmates, Roghani 2,500, mere microcosms compared with the 27,000 in Shadaye and the 100,000 around Nasir Bagh. A worry in government and the security force was how to tell apart the shepherd from the intending terrorist in the 4,000 black tents of the encampment near Quetta. There were, in fact, some alternatives to the camp crowds in Pakistan. More fortunate asylum seekers were able to live in unenclosed hamlets and even take a job in a nearby town like Peshawar or even set up a small business there, so contributing to some extent to the economy of their host country. Some alleviation was possible by mid-November 2001, as Taliban were hastily evacuating the beleaguered city of Kabul and retreating southwards in disarray. Whether or not it was the loss of dignity or the glimpse of an escape route, many thousands of Afghans now left their camps and moved towards their old homes, passing on their way an exit from Afghanistan of those who would trust nobody to ensure their safety.

November 2001 was to set a seal on a difficult year and offer some hope of redress. Afghan leaders went off to Germany at a UN invitation and there put together in the Bonn Agreement a scheme for an interim multi-ethnic administration for Kabul. A respected Afghan, Hamid Karzai, assumed office as provisional head with the likelihood that after six months he would be elected to the country's presidential chair. Peacekeepers, 4,500 from seventeen UN member states, moved into the liberated north and centre of Afghanistan. Large supplies of food were delivered by a World Food Programme convoy. Further off, in Tokyo, the UN was convening a Ministerial Conference on the Reconstruction of Afghanistan.

Was the glimmer of light in the annus horribilis of 2001 a foretaste of shining peace and progress? The blockbuster victory of UN air power and the grip of vigilant occupation had shifted out the oppressor but was neither immediate nor tangible in its consequences to allay the fears of 1 million Afghans displaced within their own country, nor did it offer any sound affirmation of security for those outside who were risking their return. The Administration's mantra of Demobilise, Disarm, Reintegrate was broadcast widely but meant little to those scratching a living on once-familiar soil. Newly installed administrators in the capital shared with UNHCR officials the need to put an end to 'warehousing', the incarceration of asylum seekers in large, insanitary camps, dependent on food handouts and rudimentary care. This was perhaps a form of quarantine, and no move towards any form of integration. Better to encourage them to step off home, into the unknown with three months' provender and a tent. The emergency camps set up just within the Pakistani border and often in isolated areas would now be launch pads for refugee flight and then they would be closed. To this end, in October 2002, a Tripartite Agreement was drawn up between Afghanistan, Pakistan and UNHCR to facilitate return over the period 2002–6. There would be 'photo-screening' to control reception numbers, a preliminary medical examination, arranged transport, and, back home, inclusion in employment-generating projects after they had found a roof over their heads. Special measures would take care of family units and vulnerable individuals. Fine in theory it must have seemed, but two nagging questions were there. Could there be any credible guarantee of safety once the refugee had landed home? And what of the future for those, no small number, who could not face up to any prospect of return?

Refugees come home: the human needs dimension

An outline of the programme for remaking Afghanistan aids understanding of a mammoth rehabilitation exercise. There were five priority measures to meet the identified needs of a peace dividend:

* Field visits by the World Bank and UN Specialised Agencies would enable costing of the programme, given that Afghanistan's internal revenues were so slight and so unreliable.

- First provisional estimates of reconstruction expenses were of the order of $15 billion over the next decade. As in other countries like post-war Cambodia, the funds would underpin so-called Quick Impact Projects and longer-term development plans.
- Communication and access to services such as roads, schools, clinics, safe water and sanitation and the demining of considerable land areas was a priority. Half of the roads must be rebuilt. Half of urban housing was in ruins.
- Feeding and health improvement of the returnees would be expensive and complex in its logistics. There had been three serious droughts and failed harvests consecutively. Afghanistan's ravaged acres could only produce enough food for six months at a time. And half of all children had been reported by the World Health Organisation as severely under-nourished.
- The sexist policies of the Taliban must be ended. Schools must do more than cater for 32 per cent of boys and only 6 per cent of girls. Correspondingly, the imbalance between male and female where women's health had been neglected must be put right.

Rehabilitation in its fullest sense must be restorative for mind and body. The World Health Organisation was estimating that 2 million Afghans were suffering from various types of post-traumatic stress disorder. Gender-based violence had incapacitated many women. Mental health service provision should include counselling and programmed psychotherapy.

Returning to a future

The most recent work with Afghan refugees is programmed through two interlinked phases, the first being to jump-start a daunting humanitarian enterprise and, second, to feed in elements of rehabilitation and integration. The first phase was to be operated through UNHCR and NGO collaboration in five major cities with outflanking sites in the camps that still remained. The essence of this most recent fieldwork is a transition from immediate life-sustaining relief to integration within a receiving community and encouraged self-help. This has to be carried through despite frequent sniping and bombing from those guerrillas still not flushed out. A following second phase represents a move from focused welfare policy, remediation rather than first aid, to development schemes that are ambitious, Afghan-controlled and expensive. Total costs will certainly reach $28 billion, it is reckoned, and there has been a first tranche from UNHCR of $185 million.

Another objective in the overall development planning is to facilitate a partnership between the public, externally aided sector, and private initiatives. In a commercial sense, the latter are still in an embryo stage.

A concluding point is that the problems of asylum seekers being addressed in contemporary Afghanistan are being styled in a new mode. No longer is it just coping with 'displacement', rather, Afghanistan (and in the eyes of UNHCR, other countries) must work out a 'regional migration strategy' which 'reflects and addresses the range of reasons beyond flight and asylum why [in this case] Afghans enter and remain in neighbouring countries'. There must be a totality of concern, in the words of UNHCR's Country Operations Plan for 2005, 'to support a transition from treating the challenge as a purely humanitarian/refugee problem under international supervision to one that can be increasingly managed as a bilateral political and economic issue by the concerned countries themselves'. Afghanistan, to quote the *Guardian* in December 2004, is still very much a country of 'warlords, poppies and slow progress', but there is every chance now that Afghans themselves will eventually decide and implement initiatives on the tortuous road from hell to something just short of heaven. The main concern has been to launch a rather tentative programme of voluntary repatriation. The major enterprise will be to handle large returning movements of Afghans waiting in Europe, together with Iraqis, and this is the issue dealt with in the following chapter.

10 The question of return

Making it home – when can we go? This is the question everybody asks, whether a single asylum-seeker, a family, or the overburdened officials at a reception point. Despite uncertainties, dramatic in their scale, many have gone home during the last few years. Globally, the figures point to a mass movement, with the 27 million asylum seekers of the 1990s peeling down through 25 million in 2001 to the 17 million of 2004. Perhaps one in three Afghans have already returned. When do they go? How will they travel? Is it safe for them to go? These are some of the issues discussed in this chapter, specifically in regard to Afghanistan and Iraq, countries from which thousands upon thousands have fled.

The return to Afghanistan: international understanding

A Memorandum of Understanding was drawn up on 12 October 2002 between representatives of the United Kingdom, UNHCR, and the Transitional Islamic State of Afghanistan. Twin objectives were to make sure that any Afghan refugee needing protection would continue to receive it and also, a practical safeguard, that what were termed the 'absorption constraints' of Afghanistan would not be hazarded by incoming numbers seeking tolerance and basic comfort.

It was resolved that cooperation between the parties was to assist voluntary, dignified, safe and orderly repatriation and successful reintegration of those in Britain who opted to return. A framework of a comprehensive programme was to be established. Afghanistan would ensure return without any fear of harassment, intimidation, persecution, discrimination or any punitive measure, save that this would not preclude the right to prosecute on account of crimes against humanity as defined in international law. A preliminary programme of information, counselling and registration would be mounted by UNHCR.

Families were to be repatriated as entire units and there would be special regard paid to vulnerable groups such as children and the handicapped. With UNHCR given full access to take care of safe travel, transit arrangements and health provision, the United Kingdom Government would meet travel costs and fully support ongoing reconstruction and rehabilitation projects. The returnees must be free to settle in their former residence or elsewhere if they so chose. An organisation working with the UN, the International Organisation for Migration (IOM), would offer all assistance on a case-by-case basis tailored to individual needs and conditions in the receiving country. Overall monitoring of the progress of repatriation would be done by a working group meeting every three months in London, Kabul or Geneva. The Memorandum also reserved the option of considering eventual forced return of unsuccessful asylum applicants.

Return schemes

In Britain the main thrust of the return scheme has been to set up the Voluntary Assisted Return and Reintegration Programme (VARRP). Funded by the Home Office and with close collaboration among a number of voluntary bodies, expert and experienced, this is a generic programme offering help to those wanting to go back permanently. The 'clients' may be those applying for asylum and awaiting decision, those whose application has been refused, or those granted exceptional leave to remain in Britain.

The London bodies, the Refugee Council and Refugee Action, published in June 2004 a detailed review of the VARRP, which had then been running for eighteen months. Much of its strength and appropriateness was derived from clear and consistent consultation, on the part of the Home Office and the Foreign and Commonwealth Office in Whitehall, with members of Afghan groups, the Red Cross, members of NGOs working in the field, legal advisory teams, academics and the media. The programme was seen as imaginative, resourceful and carefully supported. Particularly, its working lines were modifiable to suit the evolving political and security situation in Afghanistan. It was gratifying that a number of basic general principles stood firm:

- The term 'voluntary' is usually thought of in three gradations (according to UNHCR in 1996) where the first is the most consistent with values and principles of assisting agencies. Primarily, there is to be a clear and open choice by the refugee to return to the original country or stay in the host society and integrate more fully. Or, there must be a choice between return to the original country (perhaps with financial and other incentives) against staying with the host and risking forced return. Third, there must be absence of any force employed.

• Voluntary return is one of the three 'durable solutions' to the refugee situation identified by UNHCR, the others being resettlement and local integration. As a modality it is the preferred solution where (in the words of the UN General Assembly) the international community does everything possible to enable refugees 'to exercise their right to return in safety and dignity'.

• The programme approach underpins a '4R' concept (already mentioned in Chapter 2), namely, repatriation, reintegration, rehabilitation and reconstruction. These are 'linked challenges'.

The treatment of people who, after full and fair process, are found not to be refugees is not laid down in the 1951 Refugee Convention. A cardinal principle should be that voluntary return is the most desirable solution for those found not to be in need of international protection. Their right is to have access to some form of legal status and lawful residence.

The implementation of VARRP

The scheme provides advice about travel arrangements and the necessary costs and documentation for those wishing to return, together with reintegration assistance once they have reached their destination. Returnees must sign a disclaimer stating their wish to withdraw an application for asylum. Since March 2002, the IMO is helping with reintegration, so that the new entrant can find a first shelter and go on to navigate the strange intricacies of schooling, vocational training, a search for jobs, and access to health services. In respect of these 'settling in procedures' it is interesting to see the Council of Europe putting into effect agreed and concerted schemes on the same lines as the IMO. Belgium, Denmark and Luxembourg have carefully thought out projects for briefing intending leavers in focus groups. There are resettlement grants and a thoughtful plan to structure retraining projects for the skilled and professionally qualified returnees who can be expected to make a premier contribution to state recovery. The British government announced in August 2002 a cash incentive scheme, which was later termed a Resettlement Grant, offering an individual £600 and up to £2,500 for a family. Given the exigencies of travel and circumstances on landing, this does not seem a generous amount.

The programme in action offers the intending returnee several options to enlighten and strengthen personal choice. An Explore and Prepare option is designed to allow those with valid refugee status discretionary leave to return temporarily to Afghanistan to reconnoitre. Their status will not be affected thereafter. This seems an interesting proposal though it raises a number of questions as to practicality. More useful perhaps for those wrestling with the possibility of return is the opening of outreach centres, counselling workshops and legal clinics.

Afghan response to return programmes

There are clear anxieties manifest among those considering the pros and cons of a possible return home. Interviews with Afghans in Britain have shown the Refugee Council interviewing them and then the understandable confusions that cloud decision. What do we go back to? Mayhem? The return may be years away rather than immediate, for there is no alternative to a stable, peaceful, well governed homeland. Would the young ones, born thousands of miles away, be able to cope with immersion in a new culture whose ramifications and expectations are so radically strange? For the older, less robust returnee cushioned by British welfare provision there is the gnawing thought of having to forage for bare survival. As for Afghanistan itself, there is the evident lack of infrastructure and law and order in the towns, and out in the countryside the existence of pockets of warlord conflict. Could it be that this British underwriting of return possibilities is a subterfuge for lessening asylum seekers' numbers in Britain? Uncertainty about that compounds the general feeling of insecurity on every hand, both in the host society and out there in any projected returning. In any case, and whatever the direction of Afghan intentions, there is a call for accurate and timely information from trusted sources.

A concluding point is an obvious one. A get-up-and-go decision depends on rational calculation. The Refugee Council in London, knowing that one in three dispersed Afghans have gone home, has to provide the others, still in limbo, with 'pull factors' of elaborate dimensions. Among them must be policies for land and property ownership, and guidance as to employment, health and welfare provision. The information must have a future Afghanistan in mind, where industry is restored, movement is unimpeded and material progress is readily visible. Social and cultural changes will make it a very different country. At least, in contemporary perspective, it should be a country that is reasonably safe to return to.

The return to Iraq: a situation on hold

For the intending returnee, Iraq is literally a 'no go area'. For twenty-five years, UNCHR has been involved with mass movement out of a country twice seared by war in 1991 and 2003. A rough reckoning today by the United States Committee for Refugees estimates a mass of Iraqi exiles at over 130,000 and an internal dispersion of over 1 million. In fact, the dispersion is multi-ethnic, with Palestinians, Eritreans, Somalis, Iranians and Kuwaitis, all resident in Iraq, who have been forced to flee. The exiled have found some sort of asylum nearby in Jordan, Syria, Saudi Arabia and further still in Europe. Ten years of a battle with Iran in the 1980s, and the two later Gulf Wars episodes, and the ongoing arrest, torture and 'disappearances' under the Saddam Hussein regime have all eviscerated what was once a country of vast oil wealth and sophisticated enterprise. A society with half of its people under the age of fifteen must have been concerned with future potentials. The present scene is that of a ruined town-and-country landscape, with poverty, malnutrition and unemployment glaringly obvious. Three out of four people are completely dependent on slim handouts of government-provided rations. Violence stalks every street. In Iraq there are not now the haphazard possibilities of reasonably safe return, as in Afghanistan. Today's media presentation makes that clear.

It is puzzling that until very recently in Britain, pronouncements from Whitehall were seemingly complacent and misinformed. Much unhappiness and confusion was caused to Iraqis in Britain in the summer of 2003, when a Home Office minister, Beverley Hughes, declared, 'the situation in Iraq has now changed and it is believed that it is now time for people to begin to return to help in rebuilding'. That same summer the Coalition Provisional Authority in Baghdad lost no time in telling the UK Home Office that it was not prepared to deal with returnees. The incoming Iraqi governing administration had already established a Ministry for Displacement and Migration, with little to do by way of man management and it was they who called upon European Union states in August 2004, 'not to exact pressure on refugees or expel them [from host states] in current circumstances'. They recognised that it would be difficult to dissuade the determined minority of would-be returnees and those who dared a reconnaissance visit or 'day trippers' as one minister termed them. From Geneva, UNHCR called on London to abandon return plans. In their view, the essential benchmarks for a returning scenario were those of fundamental security, the basic services of potable water, power supplies, medical care, and effective border controls, and not one of these could be assured at the time. Additionally, there had been three years of drought. In the view of Geneva, a premature invitation to go back must be withdrawn. Iraqi exiles, including those whose asylum application has been turned down, all deserved protection in host communities.

Prospects for those who have returned

Eking it out in Iraq's bomb-blasted towns and the ravaged croplands are many thousands of what might be thought of as premature returnees and not those catered for by elaborate later return schemes. In more than seventy locations UNHCR has mounted a first aid relief programme, bringing to bear where it is most wanted some form of basic shelter, a rudimentary school system, vocational courses, health and sanitation facilities. Farmers trying their hand at recropping may request supplies of seed and fertilisers, even a small herd of cows. Difficulties in reasserting rights to buildings and fields are being dealt with by an Iraqi Property Claims Commission established in January 2004.

Compared with Afghanistan, there is an aching void in Iraq's political scene. A provisional government apparatus in Baghdad can do nothing unless it is guarded and often directed by a 24-hour armed Coalition presence. Visitors from the United States Committee for Refugees in late 2003 heard on all lips, often official as well as unofficial, a clutch of anxious queries. 'Who is in charge here?' 'What are the plans for this?' 'Whose responsibility is that?' 'When will things improve?' Uncertainty is a consequence, it is clear, of lack of direct, intelligible communication, between Coalition and Interim Government bureaucrats and ordinary Iraqis. Nor is much trust of Baghdad obvious. Have former stalwarts of the odious Baa'th Party been reinstated? Hussein's statue may have been toppled but is the post-war power structure a democratic and welcoming one? Resort to local authorities and the courts is made unfruitful in the absence of a properly functioning legal system. Are the 2 million Afghans who have come back since 2002 happy with their decision? Even their protectors have left the scene. Two terrorist attacks in August 2003 destroyed the UN headquarters in the Iraqi capital and killed some of the staff. UNHCR and UN agencies concluded that they could not operate from a fortress. Protracted violence would hamper and destroy much of their everyday routine. Elsewhere, other protectors, foreign and Iraqi, are continually being gunned down. As for the Iraqis themselves, either for those who stayed or for the returnee, there are indications that elements of the old fratricidal discrimination are likely to make coexistence problematical. A returning Christian, Kurd or Marsh Arab may encounter perhaps only a fraction of the former hostility that made life unbearable; nevertheless it may lead to intolerant treatment.

The inadvisability of Iraqi return

Contemporary Iraq is 'out of bounds'. Voluntary return arrangements have been suspended since the end of 2003. Geneva has put into cold storage a large-scale Repatriation and Reintegration Plan setting out the parameters for a large-scale return operation. The advice from UNHCR to all governments and relief agencies is clear and critical:

- States are strongly advised to suspend any forced repatriation of Iraqis until further notice.
- States are asked to postpone the introduction of measures which would encourage voluntary return.
- Iraqi asylum seekers should not be sent on to other countries in the Middle East regardless of their prior stay in or transit through those countries.
- Determination of refugee status to afford international protection needs must be clarified as soon as possible.
- Persecution in the form recognised by the 1951 Convention continues in Iraq in addition to widespread civil strife. The authorities are unable to provide effective natural protection and certain groups are targeted on the basis of real or perceived political affiliation, ethnic or religious differences. If asylum seekers are not recognised as refugees, UNHCR recommends that they be granted some form of complementary protection in keeping with the international principles of human rights.
- Potential voluntary returnees must be given reliable and up-to-date information about the situation in Iraq.

In the fullest sense, a return to Afghanistan is loaded with danger. In the case of Iraq, it is impossible in the short term. Iraq remains 'a country of the dead', a terrible example of a place unable to take back and offer asylum to thousands of unhappy exiles.

11   Refugee testimony as an aid to understanding asylum issues

Many asylum seekers have stories locked up in their hearts. Encouraged to tell of their troubles, of the reasons why they fled, and of the difficulties, almost insuperable at times, in making a new life elsewhere, they deserve to be listened to. This should help us to understand what they have gone through. This chapter presents a number of testimonies and goes on to suggest that the telling of what happened helps the story teller therapeutically.

Real lives

In Britain the Information Centre about Asylum Seekers and Refugees (ICAR), based in Kings College, London, has assembled a collection of refugees' own narratives which throw vivid light on their own experiences and the forming of relationships with carers. This assemblage is thought to constitute 'a powerful information resource for promoting asylum issues'. The testimonies make memorable reading.

The sources quoted by ICAR in a broadsheet updated in December 2004 are varied in their function as caring agencies or as reporting agencies. The reader may easily navigate through the ICAR list of websites. The Yorkshire and Humberside Regional Consortium works to bring asylum seekers and care workers into a collaborative relationship where clients are encouraged to 'talk things through', as a means of clarifying attitudes, dispelling anxieties, and offering some reassurance about the future. Barbed Wire Britain helps immigration detainees to give voice to feelings and fears. In Bath, a Centre for Psychotherapy and Counselling is concerned with 'the particular issues and sensitivities surrounding asylum seeker treatment'. Personal narratives supply forensic evidence for a rehabilitation programme. In a documentary vein, first-hand accounts can be had from the BBC's audio and visual gallery and from the *Observer* and *Guardian*. Refugee footballers have a voice in Let's Kick Racism out of Football. The Community Care Right to Refuge Campaign stoutly works to amplify the spoken assertions of persecution victims. There are online oral history interviews from such as the Museum of London, Lewisham Voices, Migrating Memories, Open Democracy My Experience, Refugee Action, the Scottish Refugee Council, the European Council on Refugees and Exiles, all with titles which might be thought of as either institutional or pressure groups. Here is a mix of care and campaigning.

Testimonies drawn upon in this chapter are culled from a number put together by the Medical Foundation for Victims of Torture (MFVT), an independent charity founded in 1985 in London. The MFVT exists to research, assemble and publish studies based on forensic medical reporting and on the first-hand evidence of their 'clients'. This reporting enables in-depth analysis of ill treatment as part of 'well-founded' persecution and forms a basis for treatment centres in London, Manchester and Glasgow. Great store is set by building up as complete a picture as possible, for the resulting medical report will often be used to support an asylum claim or to further the grounds for an appeal when an application has been disallowed. Not all refugees are harmed physically, although as victims of grievous discrimination, ill treatment and eviction, they may well be thought of as tortured mentally. With this point in mind, six varied testimonies are reproduced in this chapter by courtesy of the Foundation – Anysie from Rwanda, Fahed from Iran, Halil from Iraq, Nasrim also from Iran, the Kalendergil family from Turkey, and Mishou from Turkey, a Roma from Poland.

Anysie from Rwanda

This is a poignant story of a young woman increasingly rejected by two communities in conflict in her homeland, despite her parents separately belonging to Hutus and Tutsis. A book about the Holocaust she was given inspired her,

> to carry on, no matter how terrible things are. It taught me that even if you are the last member of your family to survive, to give up even if you want to die would be a betrayal of those that have been killed. It taught me too that I was not the first person to be hated because of my ethnic origins, and it showed me that other people have suffered more than me.

Discriminatory arrest as a young civil servant forced her into unspeakable privation. Even pigs, she said, lived better than that. Released after two months, she started work with the African Development Foundation which helped fund local cooperatives. Then, in 1994, the Hutus embarked on genocide and her home was one of the first to be targeted. Warned just in time, she fled with her children to the safety of a neighbour's house until that proved too risky and she was forced to hide in the bush. Arrested once more, she was taken to a military camp, held for a month and regularly beaten and tortured.

A job was found for her with the NGO Médecins sans Frontières but problems with the army persisted. Accused now of holding meetings to raise money for Hutu militias, Anysie was again arrested and brutalised, until a Tutsi relative was able to get her released. Driven immediately to the home of a priest, she remained hidden for nearly two years until it was safe for her to be smuggled out of the country with her children, who had been looked after by relatives.

Today, settling into a flat in south London with her two daughters and son, Anysie struggles to put the past behind her, with the help of the Medical Foundation.

'I have been able', she says in reflection, 'to tell of the things that happened to me, and get them out of my heart. Before, I thought I would be ashamed to look into the eyes of my children if I said anything about it . . . Once I thought I would rather die than leave my country, but in the end I had no choice.'

Now, she feels, there is the chance to make a contribution to society. 'Asylum brings knowledge and strength. I know the A-Z of human psychology. I want to train as a social worker, so that I can help others.'

Fahed from Iran

This young man comes from Iran's oilfield centre. He was only seventeen when he joined others asking a pressing question: how can it be that we are so poor when a share in Iran's vast natural resources could help all of us prosper? Activism of this sort earned him summary arrest and confinement in the tiniest of cells. Torture was an everyday occurrence with one bestial feature: he was rolled up inside a tyre to cascade along corridors and smash into anything in his path.

Release came after signing a guarantee that he would stop working for Arab nationalist organisations. He chose exile in several Arab countries as a journalist and university student. Even so he was under constant surveillance. Permanent exile in a safe haven would be his lot, he recalls:

It was very hard to leave my world behind. But I left because I could no longer live there. In a sense England was my last choice. That is because it is so difficult for me here – I cannot talk with my family or friends. Because of the cost and problems getting visas, they can never visit me. Here the system is different, initially everything was strange for me.

Fahed's welcome to England was anything but cordial. He landed at Heathrow and then languished for the next five months in Rochester prison, placed there by the Immigration Service for none too obvious a reason. Inside, his health was to decline significantly. In time, the Medical Foundation was able to intervene when Fahed himself had been able to make a case for appropriate treatment for spinal injury caused by torture. The fact that Fahed was able to express himself with reasonable fluency and his readiness to accept and work with treatment makes a case for close attention to what asylum seekers themselves feel they need rather than any swift categorisation by reception authorities. The Medical Foundation listened and prescribed a course of in-house physiotherapy. For the practitioner, Fahed's needs were clear.

'What we provide here', the Foundation stresses, 'is time and communication through our interpreters. We give people access to information so that they can eventually move on to self-management. We try and help them regain more confidence overall in their body.'

Listening to the asylum seeker would seem an avenue towards rehabilitation. It almost certainly depends on a mix of patience, compassion, rational objectivity and intuition. Not every asylum seeker will be able to project a comprehensible personality. Nor should the refugee ousted from home on account of standing up to oppression then be expected as an exile to sit still and say nothing. 'I can't stop working for my Arab people', was Fahed's instinctive response to the tedium of a London exile. 'I think about them and I hope for freedom – not just for my people but for all Iranians looking for democracy and human rights.' There is a dilemma there for the carer. Is the persecuted political refugee to wither in some anodyne sanctuary? To dampen down strong political convictions may make it easier to handle a person for a while but might it not replicate feelings of isolation and repression in an exile?

Halil from Iraq

Twice Halil has been a refugee from persecution. He is a Kurd, one of the Great Unwanted that Saddam Hussein wanted to disperse from

Iraq, and so he took his life in his hands and left over the hills for Turkey. Turkish police had no time for itinerant Kurds and resorted to beatings and water dousing rather than patient interrogation as a prelude to his being kicked out into the streets of Ankara. Safety was reached one day hidden in the back of a lorry pulling away from one of the English Channel ports. Halil, wife, daughter and son spent a cramped year with London relatives until they decided to ask the National Asylum Support Service (NASS) for possible rented accommodation. Glasgow, they were told, was a possibility. That was the place where another Kurd had been stabbed a week previously.

The flat they were offered was on an estate where racial conflict was constant. Halil's family soon became the target for abuse and violence and the police decided to move the family to a hotel until safer housing could be procured. Too terrified to stay in Glasgow, the family took matters into their own hands and, yet again, sought sanctuary in London. Halil's appeal to the NASS for help with housing brought the uncomfortable reply that they had to go back to Glasgow. The counsellors at NASS had such caseloads that they had insufficient time to listen carefully to client wishes. It was the Medical Foundation that was able to work with the severe post-traumatic stress of Halil, his wife and daughter. Tearfully, the daughter insisted through an interpreter, 'I would rather be dead. It wasn't as though we were singled out. We knew of many asylum seekers there who had experienced similar problems.' To be sent back would be too much of a nightmare to consider.

Once more, listening to asylum seekers, we are presented with a dilemma. Do we send back those unhappily housed and temporarily removed, with an assurance that things can be improved? Housing and rehousing has to be done cost-effectively. Glasgow ought to have its quota of asylum seekers. How far can the individual, psychological manifestations of individuals be allowed to have a bearing on housing allocations? In Halil's case the law appears to have listened to the plight of Halil and family when a judge ordered NASS to stop trying to force the family back to Glasgow. In any case, as the Medical Foundation realistically observes, there are pragmatic reasons why some easily reached and not too crowded places are chosen for reception housing and where the 'assignees' are expected to settle.

'Forty thousand asylum seekers', according to the Foundation's regional development coordinator,

> have so far been dispersed to places where accommodation is cheap and available – in other words, to places where no-one else wants to live. It has not been thought through strategically. If you look at the

10 most deprived boroughs in Britain outside London, you will see a mirror image of the 10 boroughs that have received the most asylum seekers. As a result, local people suffer when local resources get overstretched, and asylum seekers suffer when the locals get angry.

Resettling asylum seekers is a formidable operation. Housing agencies attempt to take account of preferences, attitudes, hopes and expectations, as the above three testimonies have shown. The exigencies of time and place make it unlikely that many asylum seekers will receive made-to-measure consideration. In interview most of the dispossessed reveal little of the thoughts that they would consider crucial to decisions. The testimonies quoted above do give some depth to what are generally superficial and often hasty interrogations.

Nasrin from Iran

The last testimony in this chapter, that of Nasrin from Iran, is the product of a most interesting project in the hands of the Medical Foundation. Refugee stories are to be processed, they say, through writing as a form of release and therapy. Clients come to the Foundation's ploy of *Write to Life* for many reasons.

> Some of them write to let the world know what is happening in their country, others to tell their own story, to get some distance by expelling the ghosts out of their heads and on to the page. Still others write because they are natural writers, in poetry, prose or short story form.

The project was begun by Sonja Linden, now writer-in-residence at the Foundation, and is now run by novelist and screenwriter Sheila Hayman, who has most kindly permitted reproduction of some of the work. In Miss Hayman's words, the aims of the project are carefully creative:

> We offer one-to-one sessions with the volunteer help of professional writers to guide and support the writing process. The first stage is inevitably a talking stage and, importantly, a time to develop mutual trust. Then there is choosing which stories to write up. A first draft is produced, sometimes with ease as the story flows out, sometimes with difficulty because of the painful nature of the memories. Finally comes the crafting stage, at which point some distancing from the story comes into play. Crafting . . . may take the form of transmuting a raw chunk of autobiography into a honed short story.

The *Write to Life* project also offers fortnightly writing group sessions: 'The spontaneity, the supportive atmosphere, and sharing attitudes or memories with people from very different places can be a hugely enjoyable distraction from the constant shuttle between a painful past and a difficult present.' By creating coherence out of an incoherent life, Miss Hayman believes, writing helps us all to envision, and make real, a better future.

Nasrin's story came alive with the help of the Write to Life project. An Iranian dental nurse, she served an eight-year prison sentence after being found guilty of promulgating civil rights. Now, in England, she finds release after years of incarceration and torture in completing a novel, *Beneath the Narcissus*. Her memories of the torture she endured are graphic:

> I hear the crack of the whip and suddenly something heavy hits the soles of my feet. They burn terribly. Again the crack of the whip and lashes hit the soles of my feet one after another. With every hit, my body trembles like a leaf that has become captured in a whirlwind. It's as if it's not my body. I am engulfed in pain.

She admits to a sense of fulfilment in completing degrees in international relations and psychology and in embarking on Ph.D. research into the psychological effects of Islamic rule in relation to women.

Does writing about your horrific experience confer a sense of real freedom? Nasrin is not so sure:

> My freedom from prison walls did not translate into real freedom; not because Iran is itself one big prison or because I was unable to write, but because I thought I would not be able to bring on paper, everything – all the regime's crimes, my own inexperience and the rottenness of some protest traditions – which had surrounded me. Freedom from my cell did not free my spirit. The rage which had gradually accumulated over eight years needed a lot longer to be released. Freedom from prison's negative effects was a huge challenge.

It was the Medical Foundation's *Write to Life* project that helped Nasrin restore a sense of coherence to an almost shattered life. Writing about her imprisonment and torture was a painful experience but in time something that was to assuage the pain. When she thought of the experience of prison, writing about it became a liberating experience. She was advised to put the account into the present tense to create a powerful sense of immediacy. That way her counsellor hoped that the present and the future would triumph over the terrors of the past.

Yet, writing the book was not at all easy. Nasrin had suffered so much and those memories were not easily erased. The title, *Beneath the Narcissus*, is a reference to how a group of prisoners would covertly communicate by burying small written messages beneath plants in the prison yard. The Medical Foundation *Write to Life* project, she believes, has enabled her to communicate with a wider world through a testimony which will help others to understand the travails of the asylum seeker.

A final testimony, again from the Medical Foundation, is written by one, Mitra, who in her short story, 'Playing Cat and Mouse', lays bare the anguish that an asylum seeker feels when she encounters hostility and ignorance in what should be a new land of the free. A number of quotations from the story powerfully illustrate a meeting with harassment:

> Leaving the tube station, I wonder which way to take. The short cut across the park and reach home soon, or the main road and avoid the woman who has been harassing my two children and me for almost a month . . .
>
> I escaped my country because it was not safe and it was too dangerous to challenge the authorities. Now, in a safe country, I am accepting the authority of this mad woman! I feel very sad and humiliated.
>
> It started almost a month ago, a few months after our arrival in London. One morning when I was taking the children to school, a woman in her late thirties came towards us and shouted harshly, 'Go home bloody foreigners! Get lost.'
>
> My first reaction was disbelief. But as she repeated it in the following days, I tried to talk to her on several occasions when my children were not with me. I intended to explain to her why I had come to her country and why I could not go back to mine. But she would not listen to me. She even spat at me . . .
>
> Going to the police was out of the question. I was an asylum seeker and did not want to create any problems. People who crossed the park were the other alternative. But they were too involved in themselves. They even passed by without saying a word when they witnessed the woman harassing us . . .
>
> Whenever the weather was good and we had enough time, we took the main road, and when we had to go through the park, we played a game of cat and mouse . . .
>
> We've come here to have a safe and peaceful life. We haven't done anybody any harm. Why doesn't this woman leave us alone? Why can't I stop her from harassing us? I've always been a good fighter in my life. Why am I so weak and passive now? Who has

taken my confidence away? This crazy, racist woman, those who do not see me and treat me as an invisible object, or the welfare officers who make me feel ashamed of asking for something that is every human being's right?

Mitra's agonising over hostility is finally soothed when she enlists the help of a young man who, apologising for the outrageous incidents, promises to talk to the offender coming now towards them and to make sure that the family's walk will never be menaced again.

Mitra realises only too well that her battle for a life with dignity continues even outside her homeland. Now, things are to be different. They can finish their walk through the park without any fear this time.

A refugee family's fatal error

Occasionally, testimonies reveal that some asylum seekers are no strangers to the most macabre of experiences. An instance of this is the Medical Foundation's account of a fatal error that condemned the Kalendergil family from Turkey. Their story is told by Kadriye Kalendergil, a middle-aged mother and the family's sole survivor. An account of what they went through exemplifies the extraordinary risks many asylum seekers are forced to run when seeking exile, risks that counter the frequent assertions that those who are striving to reach Britain are driven not by desperation, rather, they are looking for an easy life at our expense. Also exemplified is that the act of flight itself can bring its own trauma, whether it is the sudden death of a family member or of a companion or whether it is rape by a border guard as the price of a safe passage. Traumatic, too, is the all too common intimidation and extortion of traffickers.

The Kalendergil story is told by the Foundation in these words:

> An error made when the Kalendergils were trying to cross the Channel triggered their tragedy. The family, Turkish Kurds, were among a group of 13 refugees who, in Belgium, were hidden away in a container full of office furniture for a voyage it was expected to take hours.

But the people smugglers, or agents, organising the clandestine run chose a container heading not for the UK, but for Ireland. Instead of hours, it was at sea for days. Watertight, it was also airtight, and by the time it was opened on a business park outside Wexford, it was a coffin. Eight of the occupants had suffocated.

Kadriye, 40, who was rescued comatose can't bring herself [now] to speak of the horror that engulfed the lives of her husband Hasan, 45, and their children 15-year old Kalender, and Zelide, aged 10, late in 2001.

She has described, however, the reasons the family left their home in Istanbul. 'I was not happy about leaving, but we had no choice', she explained through a Medical Foundation interpreter, 'My husband had been detained for a month because of his support for the Kurds, and tortured, while at school my son was harassed because he was Kurdish'.

The Kalendergils were farmers in southeast Turkey. They were forced from their fields by Turkish security police emptying village after village in their harrying of Kurd separatists. Making a living in Istanbul, as street traders, earned the family some respite until secret police rounded them up and arrested Hasan for beating and jail. At his eventual release it was decided that they should all contact an agent who would arrange an expensive but supposedly safe passage to the UK.

The outcome of all this suffering has brought little comfort to Kadriye in her North London flat. There is only one picture on the walls, that of the Kalendergils. She will say little of what took place in transit. Her brother, also now an exile in Britain, has had to learn what happened from one of the other survivors, who told him of the hell they had had to endure: 'It was pitch black inside and those inside tried to raise the alarm by banging on the walls. Some of the younger people tried to make an airhole, but they became breathless very quickly. The children were screaming and fainting.'

The transit agents were prosecuted in Belgium early in 2003. Seven of them were given jail sentences of up to ten years for what the court said was the 'unintentional manslaughter' of the eight dead. The court heard that it was believed the refugees had been locked in the container for at least nine days.

Kadriye has been referred for psychotherapy. A consultant believes this will be most beneficial. 'We will be able to help her', it is thought, 'once she is able to engage in a therapeutic process. Like a number of Medical Foundation clients, it is her experiences while fleeing into exile that have fundamentally traumatised her.'

A child refugee no longer in fear

Last, there is the testimony of a young Roma girl from Poland, now living in London. Her experience of ethnic hatred and aggression has been enough to cripple her for life emotionally and she is only recently being helped towards normality.

Roma, or Gypsies, have a distinctive culture and values and rituals rooted in a strong sense of family loyalty. For centuries, however, they have met with the prejudice and aggressive behaviour of their detractors. These are circumstances that made life difficult in their places of origin. It is distressing, though, that having made their way to some sort of asylum they continue to meet hostility in the host communities of Europe. A contemporary epithet directed at them in some British newspapers labels them as 'bogus asylum seekers'. They are said to be dishonest, troublesome interlopers.

Mishou was born in a small Polish country town and lived there until she was seven. Things were loving and good at home, unpleasant in the street, at school, and in shops. There were times when her parents were set upon, beaten up and injured. There was the hideous night when a group of thugs came to torch the family home. No more could be sustained and the family, reluctant to leave elderly relatives behind, embarked for Britain.

Exile in London for Mishou's family got off to an unpromising start when an initial application for asylum seeker status was turned down. There were months of uncertainty and distress before an appeal succeeded. Somehow, the family had to try to comfort a daughter who could not sleep at night and who, during the day, was sometimes frozen in fear at the thought that they would be forced to go back to Poland. Mishou's agonised state called for prompt and intensive medical surveillance and treatment. A psychological report put her condition in very plain terms:

> Mishou has clearly been cumulatively traumatised by several experiences since her earliest years. She was and still is terrified that she will be killed and that the adults in her life will be taken away from her. Her dreams are repetitive and are about abuse in the streets, abuse in school, violence towards her father, violence towards the Roma community and towards family property.

It was in the light of findings such as these that the Home Office allowed the family to stay in Britain.

It is difficult for the youngest asylum seekers to find words to describe their experiences of care, comfort and toleration being harshly denied them. Their testimonies lack depth and shape undoubtedly because their verbal resources are slim. The Medical Foundation is just one of a number of groups in Britain working with people like Mishou to alleviate past suffering by offering them the chance of a present and a future in which they can live happily. Creative work in art, drama, music and storytelling aims at helping children to 'make boundaries between past and present, internal and external experiences'. Hopefully, in time, children and adolescents will develop emotional strengths instead of feeling passive and helpless and victims of malevolence. Adolescent refugees who have experienced political or ethnic violence frequently appear anxious that the troubles they have undergone in the past may recur. Work with them on themes of social, cultural and physical identity is held to be central to reducing such anxieties.

No alternative but to leave

Can those of us living in daily comfort and security really comprehend the turmoil in the minds of asylum seekers? Spoken testimonies, where the words can be found, provide an inkling of what has been faced and endured. The narratives in this chapter from the MFVT have an element of 'torture' in the experience and the point has been made that, apart from physical abuse, the distress and agony of decision, transit and even of uncertain reception can well be spoken of as mental torture.

Not one of the six storytellers quoted had any alternative but to leave. Anysie, in Rwanda, was menaced from all sides of a splintered society. She had to leave. She now feels that the experience of seeking asylum brought her knowledge and strength, something she would like to employ as a social worker.

The Iranian, Fahed, found no security at first in neighbouring Arab countries. Nor did Britain welcome him at first until his own insistence and medical intervention earned him priority. Fahed's position poses a question to receiving authorities. Is an asylum seeker permitted to exercise strong political convictions in a land of exile? Is this something he should have left behind when asylum is to be regarded as neutral territory? Might the Iranian government have a case for accusing the United Kingdom of harbouring dissidents and allowing free voice to anti-Iranian sentiments?

Halil from Iraq and his family found neither peace nor security in Glasgow. They took refuge in London. The National Asylum Support Service needs to fill cheap and easily available housing allocations and they instructed Halil to go back to their intolerable Glasgow estate. It took a judge to rescind the instruction and save the family from a traumatic plight.

Storytelling for the asylum seeker is seen to offer therapeutic possibilities for those who are able, with some assistance, to express themselves. Nasrin, from Iran, has been helped to distance herself from the past and to find more coherence in the present and future. Free of persecution, she went on to complete university studies and to set about writing a novel. Nevertheless, she feels, she has not yet attained the full sense of 'real freedom'.

There is an element of the *Grande Guignol* in the suffering of the Kalendergil family. For them, pitched out of Istanbul, there was the unexpected hell of a voyage, locked in a box, lasting days rather than hours. Prosecution of traffickers for 'unintentional manslaughter' was how the courts saw it. Readers of this narrative will have other considerations, moral ones, in mind, and wonder how trafficking can be stamped out.

Lastly, the Polish girl, Mishou, never knew peace and security outside her own home. As with Fahed, when the story was coaxed out of them, there was a need for urgent rehabilitation which plain immigration procedures were unable to address.

12 Retrospect

Writing about asylum seekers and refugees inevitably links past, present and future. Issues and problems raised span this timescale. There are two parts to this retrospective chapter. First, a brief resumé of preceding chapters stressing the most significant features and then a list of suggested issues that are worth consideration, further discussion and enquiry. It is hoped that this will help readers grope their way through the public fog of inadequate information and frequent prejudice.

Resumé

The first chapter dealt with problems of distinguishing bona fide refugees from other asylum seekers. The reference point of 1951 focused on 'well-found fear of persecution' as a criterion for refugee assistance with strong post-war instincts underpinning measures for protecting, repatriating and integrating the displaced people of mainly a shattered Europe. Sixty years or so later there is a case for redefinition in a world that is shaping very differently.

Chapter 2 considered the scale and diversity of asylum seeking. There was a brief glance at the 'march of millions' in historical context. Then, given that concern and compassion, in worldwide terms, has led to protective action on a grand scale, there followed a discussion of protection principles and of restorative action.

Asylum seekers and refugees in the United Kingdom were next dealt with where the government was attempting to cope with major numbers and with the resulting problems of reception procedures, application formalities, legal approaches and the logistics of accommodation, resettlement and community assimilation. The very obvious web of fallacy and confusion was looked at. The intricacies of process and reform were seen as constantly debated in Whitehall, in Parliament and among NGOs, and then variously translated in action.

A chapter on Europe outlined cycles of explicit humanitarian concern with the encouragement of immigration, then some falling back to quotas, then the beginnings of tougher controls, then the much harder-nosed imposition of restrictions and recourse to deterrence. Lately, the twenty-five members of the European Union have been moving towards 'harmonisation' of policies and procedures. Nevertheless, lack of standardisation and safeguards in treatment of asylum pleas opened the field for traffickers and exploiters. At a rather late date, European governments are seen as now being keener to work out high protection standards and to consider sponsoring developmental schemes in the developing world that may help stem the flow of the oppressed.

The global work of UNHCR was the topic of a chapter which told how the initial concern mainly with a Europe tottering out of war was given eventually a broader, universal remit. In the course of a half-century's enterprise, the UN agency was seen to be cooperating with governments and NGOs in a range of partnerships, with protective measures which incorporate relief as well as rescue. The years had inevitably yielded much debate and controversy where a multinational organisation has had to forge instruments for dealing with states' sovereign interests and with their agendas and priorities.

Four case studies were presented to illustrate the wide variety of asylum searching and, indeed, the great difficulties in resolving problems and equable treatment. As a group these studies throw up urgent questions. What can those outside a locale in conflict do to forestall on-going displacement of people? How far does external intervention breach autonomous sovereignty? Is it possible that offering, as it were, life rafts to asylum seekers emerging from the Balkans or Rwanda goes some way to meeting ethical principles without being able to put a stop to wholesale violation of human rights? The instance of the Palestinian refugees was an example of many years of exile and dispute as to any sort of reparation. The conflict of which they are victims had deep roots where all parties saw themselves as having the Right to Belong and the Right to Return and where the claims and counter-claims appeared irremediable. International mediation had sought political solutions without any evident success. Meanwhile, many of the Palestinians languished in refugee camps.

The chapter on Balkan refugees described the terrorising and expulsion of civilians where there were vigorous ethnic contests (deemed insupportable by most world opinion). Intensive mediation and spasmodic UN peacekeeping seemed merely to provide a presence rather than powerful assistance. Europeans as a whole had to keep their

generosity and any help in the field at a distance and minister to a drip
flow of those who could escape. The provision, by would-be 'saviours',
of camps and 'safe havens' was not successful and raised questions of
practicality and humanitarian intervention, both strategic and tactical.

A following chapter on Rwanda pitched 'killing fields' in horrific
terms similar to what was seen in Pol Pot's Cambodia. A society,
completely bisected, expelled a flood of refugees who now, to the
amazement of some, were prepared to return from sanctuary in neighbouring countries. Critical questions here focused on the willingness
and ability of Rwandans themselves to resuscitate a united society. The
midwife in this process of regeneration was UNHCR, assisted by
NGOs. Prospects for returnees were indeed questionable. In what ways
could they be helped to survive?

A case study of the refugee situation in Afghanistan was always
going to throw up disturbing problems. A destructive cycle of war,
intolerant regime, and war again, would decimate a country and
explode the hopes of any who fled and thought of return. Yet nearly
half of the 6 million who fled the invading Red Army and then the
fanatical utopia of the Taliban ultimately went back. Today's anxiety
concerned the extent to which returnees could be rehabilitated by a
society, as in Rwanda, and the Balkans, that had been fractured,
terrorised and only just rescued.

The Question of Return was the main piece of a chapter returning
to the themes of the main text. In general terms, there were numerous
carefully thought-out and well designed repatriation programmes,
some of them perhaps crafted with the expediency of immigrant
removal in mind. An instance of an ambitious approach to repatriation was the Voluntary Assisted Return and Rehabilitation Programme
put together by a caucus of governmental and non-governmental
experts in Britain, together with delegates from UNHCR and, in this
instance, from Afghanistan. Design, implementation and Afghan
response were surveyed as a guide to what might or might not be done
when refugees indicated a willingness to go home. The chapter
concluded with the ominous point that a return to present-day Iraq
had been deemed 'inadvisable'. The situation there was 'on hold'.

Personal testimonies of refugees featured in the next to last chapter.
This was thought to be a useful means of depicting what some
refugees had gone through and what they encountered on arrival in a
host state. Readers would perhaps find this chapter unsettling, with its
accounts of inconsistency of treatment on reception and, worse still,
some of the problems the newly arrived experienced as they went
among their 'protectors'. Implicit here, in the words newcomers them-

selves used, was turmoil and distress. This was often coped with bravely thanks to the understanding and help of others, but it did put to us the question of how effective and how coherent were we making reception, processing and integration procedures?

In retrospect, and quite dramatically, as the safety of a host land is secured, the linking of past, present and future appears realised starkly by the refugee. A fitting last line for these chapters takes up the words of the Refugee Council that there must be for seekers after asylum a need to bury the past, to face up to the present, and to go on to 'reclaim a future'. For observers of the Human Flood there is also an obligation to merge time-frames. Asylum seeking is multi-variate. It poses inescapable issues – of need, scale, duration, of human response. Is there not a doubled urge on the part of migrant and host, the twofold impulse (in Kofi Annan's words) 'to integrate while retaining their identity'?

Issues for discussion

A dozen issues are listed here, a brief selection of points dealt with in earlier chapters. They are among the things that deserve reflection and further exploration, ideally in group discussion. Readers looking for more information on specific topics will be able to navigate some of the internet sites and organisational addresses listed in the Where to Find Out More section that follows or by using keywords in internet search engines.

1   'The values of the [1951 Refugee] Convention are timeless', yet it was now time 'to stand back and consider its application in today's world' (Prime Minister Tony Blair to House of Commons, 2002). How so? Is there a contradiction here?

2   'Do not think of them [refugees] in the bureaucratic language of "decisions" and "declarations" and "priorities" . . . I entreat you, think of the human beings who are touched by your decisions. Think of the lives who wait on your help' (Vaira Vika-Feiberga, 2001). This statement touches the heart but in what terms would you put it to hard-pressed immigration officials?

3   'When you consider a definition think what it tells you about the definers'. This is a well-worn aphorism but it may advance reflection.

4   How do we, on the outside, help those on the inside who are being maltreated and displaced? (A situation we have faced in Cambodia, Bosnia, Rwanda, Angola, Sudan, to name just a few. What are the possibilities of preventive action?)

5   In the case of voluntary repatriation what guarantees of successful resettlement in the original country should be required?

6   'Asylum seekers are a threat to our future' (*Mail on Sunday*, 2 March 2004). True or not true?

7   'We can no longer believe anything the government says and we have no faith in its figures' (*Daily Express*, May 2004). What do we do to get the true picture?

8   'Globality of concern' appears to be moving today towards 'guarded concern'. Is this reflecting 'Them' and 'Us' defensiveness in many countries?

9   'The long occupation has succeeded in changing us from children of Palestine to children of the idea of Palestine' (Mourid Barghouti, 2004). In what ways might Israel as a potential receptor see the return of this thoughtful Palestinian refugee as an unwelcome prospect? Is similar political latency liable to be a handicap to reception elsewhere?

10   The Explore and Prepare option encourages potential returnees to visit Afghanistan on preliminary reconnaissance. Is this a practicable option? What would they learn of the present and of the future?

11   Refugee aid agencies often found it insuperable to work alongside the military involved in conflict, for instance, in Kosovo, Iraq and Afghanistan. The army was the only organisation able to provide effective security. In what ways would it be preferable for such agencies to work on the periphery of a conflict rather than at the centre?

12   'Freedom from my cell did not free my spirit' (Nasrin, 2003, in the Medical Foundation's *Write to Life* project). Could it be that liberation from persecution or oppression is merely a preliminary stage in feeling free? What more might a receiving community do by way of rehabilitation?

Postscript

As this book was going to press, the British Home Secretary, Charles Clarke, launched on 8 February 2005 a government five-year immigration and asylum seeker strategy. There was an acknowledgement that tourists, students and migrant workers make a vital contribution to a vibrant United Kingdom economy and so there was a need to make sure that their skills and talents benefit Britain over against the importance of preventing illegitimate abuse of hospitality and refuge.

The British proposals are described here as an example of an approach to migration management by a receptor state in the developed world. The lines of this approach are being studied particularly carefully in France, Germany, and the Netherlands.

The government measures are comprehensive in four main areas and are listed below only in outline:

I Migration

A four-year points system for entry applicants replaces the current work permit scheme.

Tier One – Highly skilled migrants, including engineers, doctors, IT experts, will be able to enter the UK without existing job offers. Points are to be based on qualifications, work experience and current salary. Extra points can be accrued for shortage skills.
Tier Two – Skilled migrants (with A-level equivalent at least) such as administrators, teachers, nurses. Entrance is allowed if jobs are already offered and if otherwise the employer cannot find the skills within the European Union.
Tier Three – Low-skilled migrants. The present quota-based scheme for non-European Union nationals in agriculture, hospitality, food processing will give way to tighter, small-scale quotas in specific

shortage areas. New European Union accession states will be given preference in meeting labour demands. Tier Three workers are to leave at the end of any agreed stay and are not to be joined by dependants.

Tier Four – Generally students and workers in specialised categories who do not compete with the domestic labour force and whose stay is to be temporary with no route to settlement.

Tiers Two to Four depend upon a sponsor guaranteeing a valid application. Tiers Three and Four hinge on original countries confirming their individual emigrants' intention to return.

II Asylum

Refugees – Temporary leave to stay is to replace present permanent permission. The situation in the country of origin will be reviewed after five years to confirm safety of return.

Dealing with claimants – There will be faster tracking of asylum claims. Additional centres for those being refused asylum seeker status are to be provided together with assurance of regular reporting arrangements and electronic tagging.

Removals – New targets for removing failed asylum seekers are to be set.

Source countries – Britain will liaise with countries of failed asylum seekers to ensure they can be sent home 'by placing immigration at the heart of our relationship . . . and making clear that failure to co-operate will have repercussions, including access to some migration schemes'. Immigration detention centres will be expanded.

III Settlement and citizenship

Only skilled workers in Tiers One and Two will be able to apply for permanent settlement, after five years rather than the present four. They will have to pass tests in English Language and Knowledge of Britain. Less-skilled entrants will not gain citizenship and are to leave after five years. During that time, welfare benefits extend only to schooling and some health care.

IV Enforcement

Border controls – There will be more scrutiny of intending migrants, those already arriving, and those leaving. By 2008, foreign nationals here for more than three months will need ID cards, be fingerprinted, and have selective health checks.

People trafficking – Enforcement operations will be stepped up with on-the-spot £2,000 fines per employee on any company using illegal immigrant labour.

This strategy, termed 'Controlling our Borders: Making Migrants Work for Britain. A Five-year Strategy for Asylum Seekers and Immigrants', can be found at http://www.official-documents.co.uk/document/cm64/6472.htm

Comment

Political party opinion was mixed, with broad Labour Party support for 'managed migration' (providing opportunity rather than constituting a crisis), to Conservative approval of more stringent control, to Liberal Democrat preference still for quotas and the suggestion that an independent agency process asylum seeker claims more speedily. Press comment ranged from contempt for 'yet another set of Labour half-measures conceived in panic' to those who wondered whether any points systems could appropriately, fairly and carefully distinguish the genuine asylum seeker from the economic opportunist. Demographic questions of how many should be let in, and who they should be, rolled around with political and sociological assertions. The appropriateness of a grading system was queried by many. Is it possible for such a system to rate potential – intellect, creativity, self-reliance – the elements of a dynamic, mixed society? How would Albert Einstein and Sir Isaiah Berlin have scored in the points processing? Reservations similar to those above have been voiced in France, Denmark, Austria, and Sweden. Controversy reigns.

Where to find out more

Publications

A great deal has been written about refugees, asylum seekers and immigrants, especially during the last twenty years. Students will be able to search the literature fairly easily using internet keywords. The list below is made up of fairly recent and easily obtainable items used constantly by the author.

Alstov, P. (ed.) (1992) *The United Nations and Human Rights: A Critical Approach*, Oxford: Oxford University Press.

Amnesty International (2004) *Guidelines for Journalists on Proper Coverage of Refugee-related Topics*, published for National Union of Journalists Ethics Council.

Ashford, Mark (1993) *Detained Without Trial: A Survey of Immigration Act Detention*, London: Joint Council for the Welfare of Immigrants.

Barghouti, Mourid (2004) *I Saw Ramallah*, London: Bloomsbury.

Coker, Jane (ed.) (1998) *Promoting the Health of Refugees: Its Present State and Future Directions*, Report of Health Education Authority, Abingdon, Oxon: Marston Book Services.

Cook, Betsy (1999) Interviews at Sabra and Chatila Palestinian Refugee Camps, *Journal of Palestinian Studies*, vol. xxix, no. 1, autumn, 50–7.

Farsoun, S. and Zachara, C. (1997) *Palestine and the Palestinians*, Boulder CO: Westview Press.

Feller, Erika, Turk, Volker and Nicholson, Frances (eds) (2003) *Refugee Protection in International Law*, Cambridge: Cambridge University Press.

Ferris, Elizabeth (1993) *Beyond Borders: Refugees, Migrants and Human Rights in the Post-Cold War Era*, Geneva: World Council of Churches.

Glacaman, Rita and Johnson, Penny (2002) *Who lives in Jenin Refugee Camp. A Brief Statistical Profile*, Palestine: Birzeit University (access http://www.electronicintifada.net).

Goodwin-Gill, Guy (1996) *The Refugee in International Law*, 2nd edn, Oxford: Clarendon Press.

Gordenker, L. (1987) *Refugees in International Politics*, London: Routledge.

Hailbronner, Kay (1996) 'The right to asylum seeking and the future of asylum seeking procedures in the European Community', *Journal of International Refugee Law*, vol. 2, no. 3, 341–60.

Hayter, Teresa (2000) *Open Borders: The Case against Immigration Controls*, London: Pluto Press.

Helton, Arthur (1990) 'What is refugee protection?', *International Journal of Refugee Law*, special issue, 119–29.

——(1994) 'UNHCR and protection in the 90s', *International Journal of Refugee Law*, vol. 6, no. 1, 1–2.

Holmes, Colin (1991) *A Tolerant Country? Immigrants, Refugees and Minorities in Britain*, London: Faber.

Joly, Daniele (1996) 'Haven or Hell?', *Asylum Policies and Refugees in Europe*, London: Macmillan.

Kissinger, Henry (1982) *Years of Upheaval (1973–77)*, New York: Little, Brown.

Knox, Catherine (1997) *Credit to the Nation: A Study of Refugees in the United Kingdom*, London: Refugee Council.

Kushner, Tony, and Knox, Catherine (2001) *Refugees in an Age of Genocide*, London: Frank Cass.

Loescher, Gil (2001) *The UNHCR and World Politics: A Perilous Path*, Oxford: Oxford University Press.

Loescher, Gil, and Monahan, Laila (eds) (1989) *Refugees and International Relations*, Oxford: Oxford University Press.

Manning, Patrick (2005) *Migration in World History*, London: Routledge.

Marrus, Michael (1985) *The Unwanted: European Refugees in the Twentieth Century*, Oxford: Oxford University Press.

Mayotte, Judy A. (1992) *Disposable People: The Plight of Refugees*, New York: Maryknoll.

Morris, Benny (2003) *The Birth of the Palestinian Refugee Problem Revisited*, Cambridge: Cambridge University Press.

Nicholson, Frances, and Twomey, Patrick (eds) (1999) *Refugee Rights and Realities: Evolving International Concepts and Regimes*, Cambridge: Cambridge University Press.

Ogata, Sadako (1994) 'The evolution of UNHCR', *Journal of International Affairs*, vol. 47, no. 2, 419–28.

Oxfam (2001) *Asylum: The Truth Behind the Headlines*, Report from the Oxfam Poverty Programme in Scotland re. press coverage, Oxford: Oxfam.

Refugee Council – numerous publications including a monthly *In Exile*. London SW8 1BR.

Roberts, Adam (1998) 'More refugees, less asylum: a regime in transformation', *Journal of Refugee Studies*, vol. 11, no. 6, 379ff.

Rutter, Jull (2004) *Refugees: We Left Because We Had To*, London: Refugee Council (Citizenship teaching resource for 11–18 years).

Said, Edward (1994) *The Politics of Dispossession: The Struggle for Palestinian Self-determination 1969–94*, New York: Pantheon Books.

Steiner, Niklaus, Gibney, Mark and Loescher, Gil (eds) (2003) *Problems of Protection, the UNHCR, Refugees and Human Rights*, London: Routledge.
Whittaker, David J. (1995) *United Nations in Action*, London: UCL Press.
——(1997) *United Nations in the Contemporary World*, London: Routledge.
Zieck, Caroline (1997) *UNHCR and Voluntary Repatriation of Refugees: A Legal Analysis*, Boston MA: Martinus Nijhoff.

Journals

Relevant articles appear in these journals from time to time:

Foreign Affairs
International Affairs
International Journal of Refugee Law
International Migration Review
International Relations
International Studies
Journal of International Affairs
Journal of Refugee Studies
Millennium Review of International Studies
Third World Quarterly
The World Today

Statistical resources

Britain

Constable, Jo (2002) *Asylum by numbers 1985–2000: Analysis of Available Asylum Data from* 1985–2000 London: Refugee Council.
Hanson, Randall (2000) *Citizenship and Immigration in Post-war Britain: The Institutional Origins of a Multicultural Nation*, Oxford: Oxford University Press.
ICAR (2004) Key statistics about asylum seekers in the UK. Available at http://www.icar.org.uk/res/stats/analysis.html
Immigration and asylum seekers statistics (Home Office) Available at http://www.homeoffice.gov.uk/rds/immigration.html

Europe

European Council on Refugees and Exiles (ECRE). Available at http://www.ecre.org.uk.html
Refugee Council (London) Available at http://www.refugeecouncil.org.uk
Rest of world
UNHCR (Geneva) Available at http://www.unhcr.ch
Population Data Unit and UNHCR Statistical Yearbooks

Refugee Council
Sending an email to Refugee Council and ICAR will bring back quick, less
complex answers to queries about facts and figures. For e-mail addresses
see below.

Useful websites

UNHCR: http://www.unhcr.ch
Refugee Council: http://www.refugeecouncil.org.uk
Information Centre about Asylum and Refugees, Kings College, London
(ICAR): http://www.icar.org.uk
Medical Foundation for the Victims of Torture, London: http://www.torture-
care.org.uk
Refugee Action, London: http://www.refugee-action.org.uk
Home Office, Whitehall, London (Immigration and Nationality Directorate):
http://www.homeoffice.gov.uk
United States Committee for Refugees: http://www.uscr.org

Useful e-mails

Refugee Council: Info@refugeecouncil.org.uk
ICAR. Icar@kcl.ac.uk

Useful telephone numbers for information, etc.

Refugee Council: 020 7820 3042/3060 – with contact persons or 'Assistants' in
a number of English regions, Wales and Scotland.
ICAR: 020 7848 2103.
Refugee Education Advisory Service: 071 226 6747.
Student Action for Refugees (STAR): 0171 820 3006 and info@star-
network.org.uk
Medical Foundation for Victims of Torture: 020 7697 7777.

Index